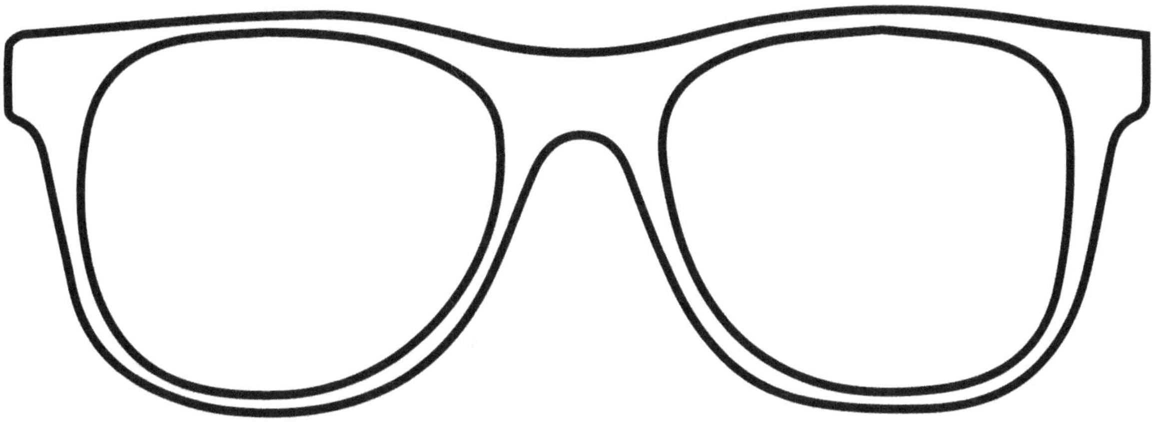

THIS BOOK BELONGS TO:

____

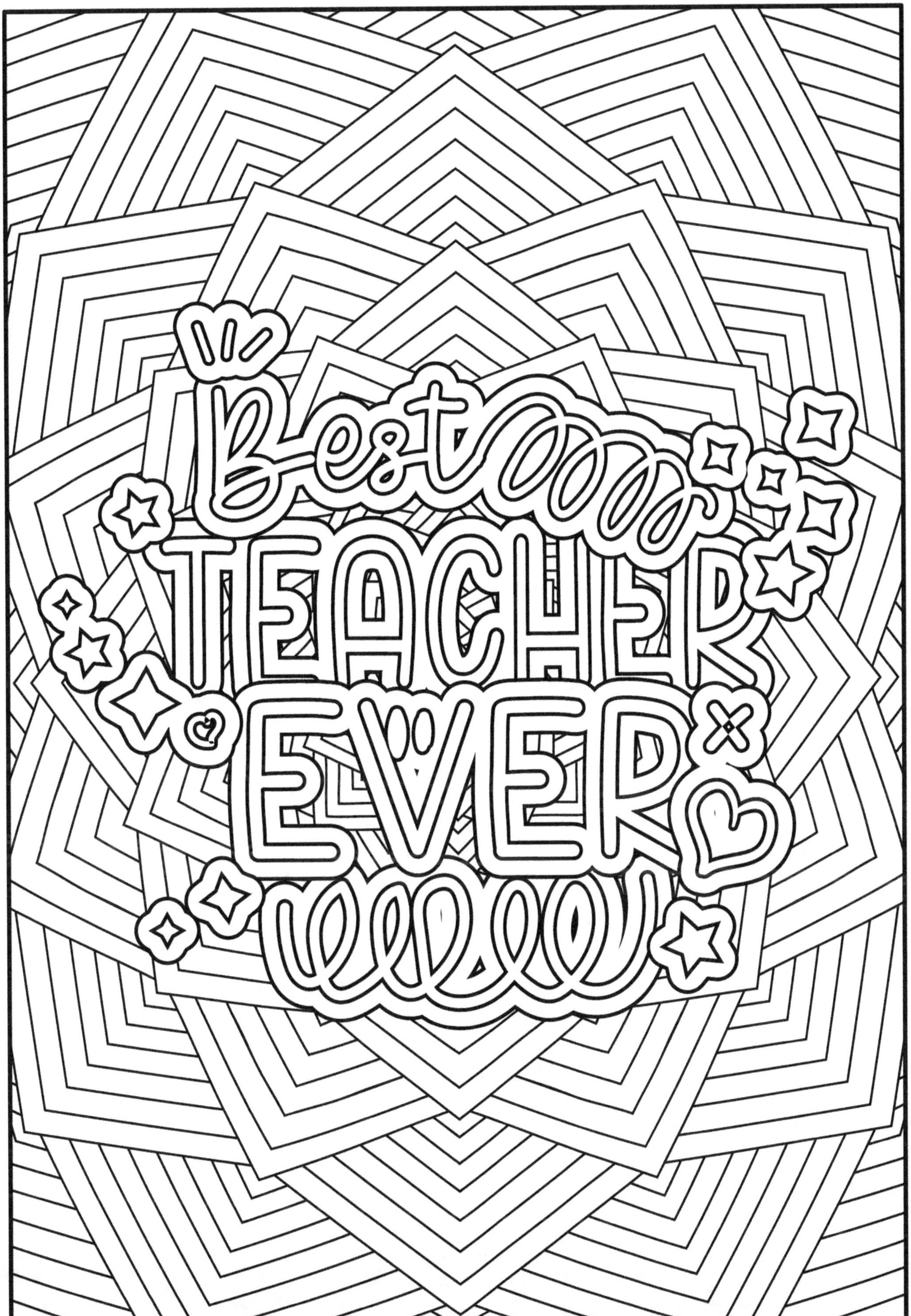
Best
TEACHER
EVER

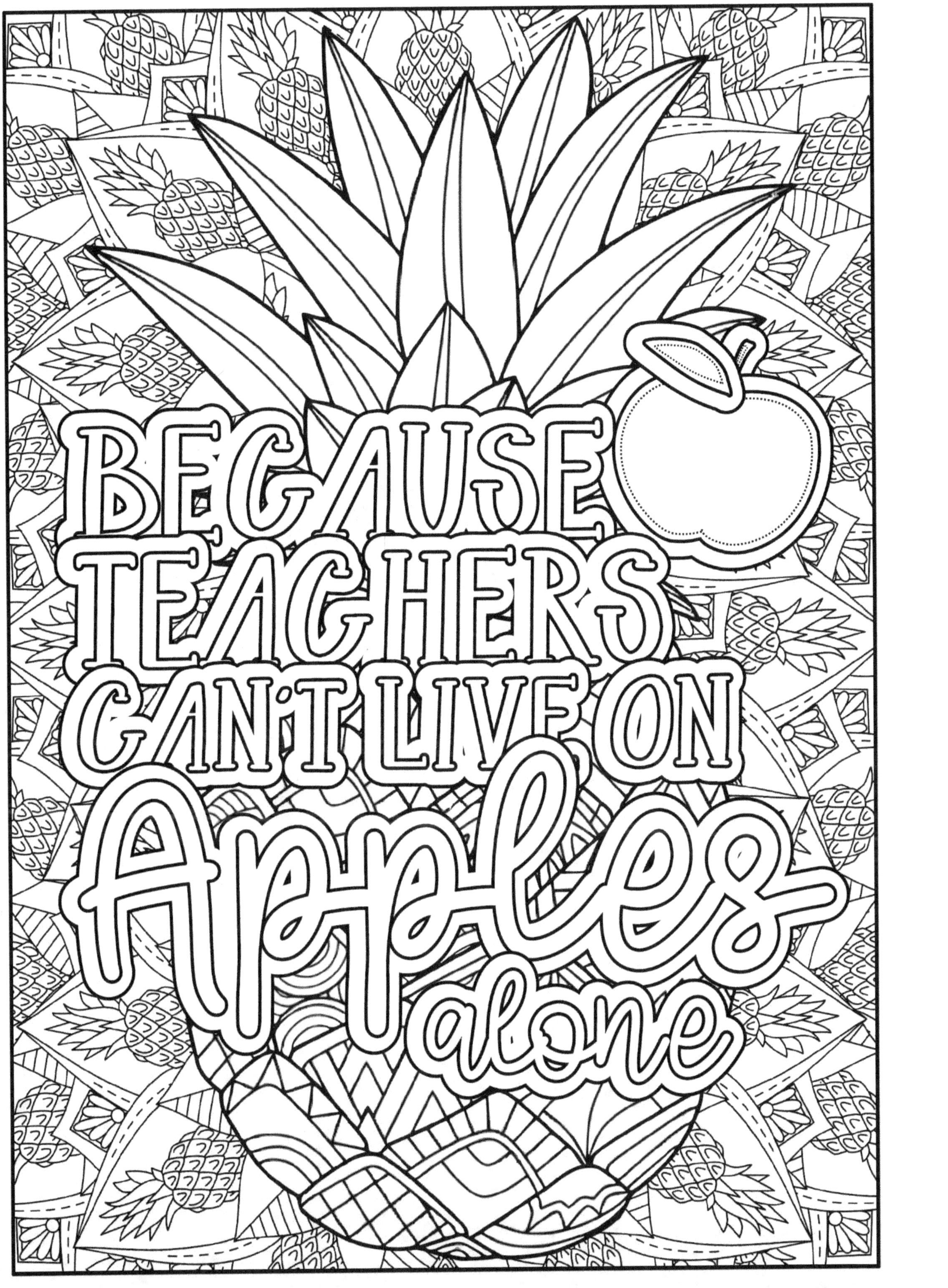
BECAUSE TEACHERS CAN'T LIVE ON
Apples
alone

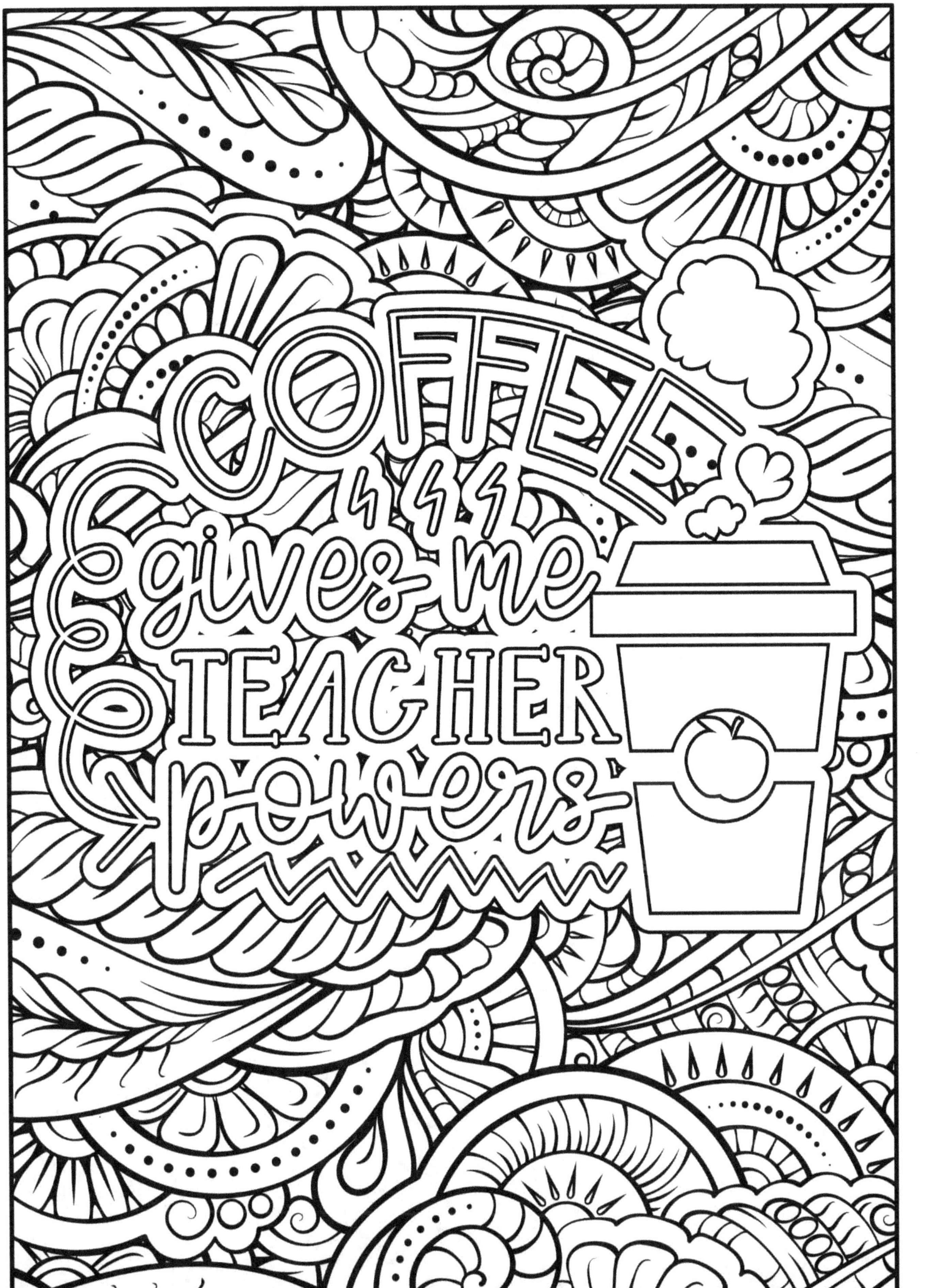
Coffee
gives me
TEACHER
powers

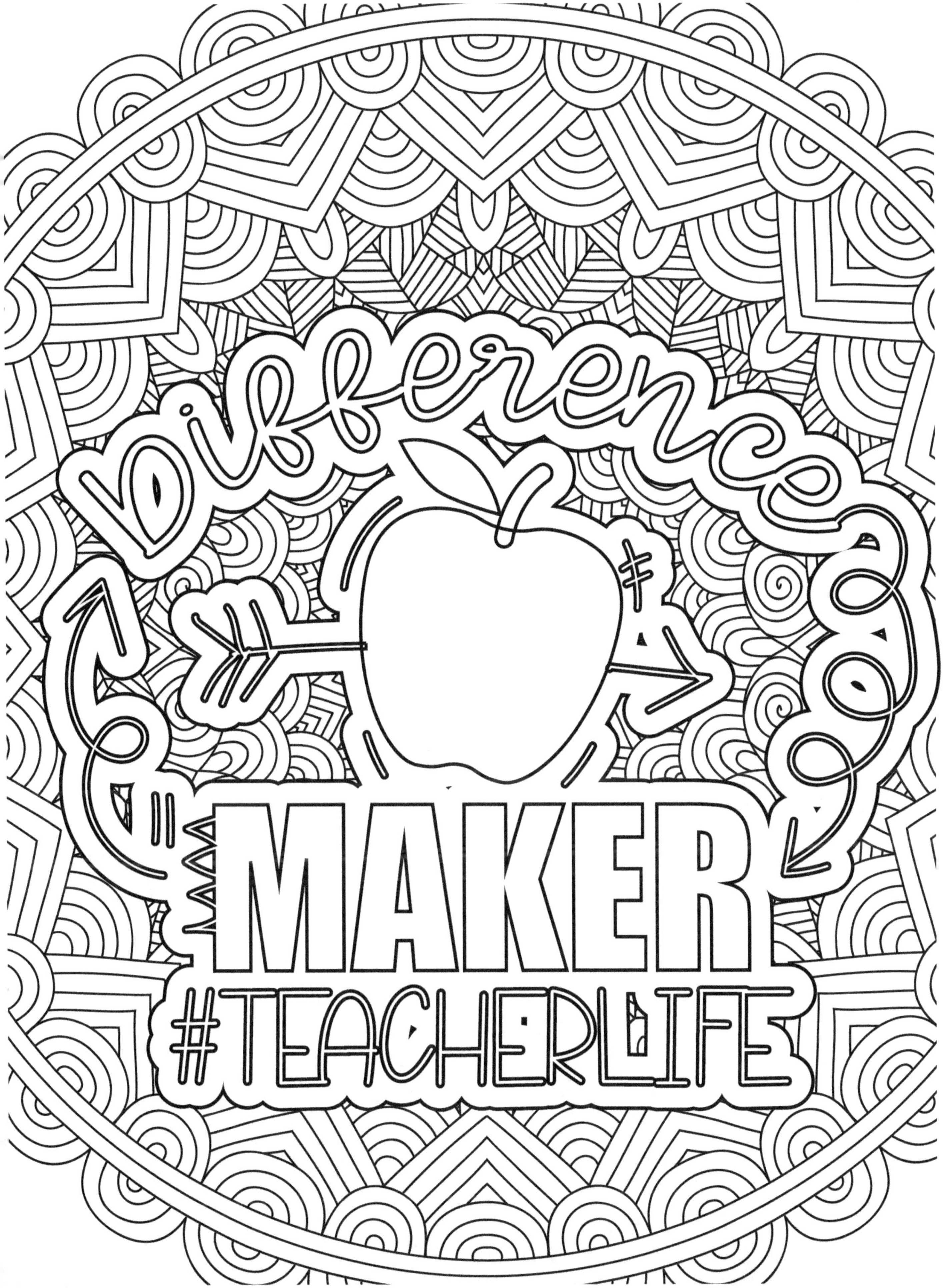
Difference
MAKER
#TEACHERLIFE

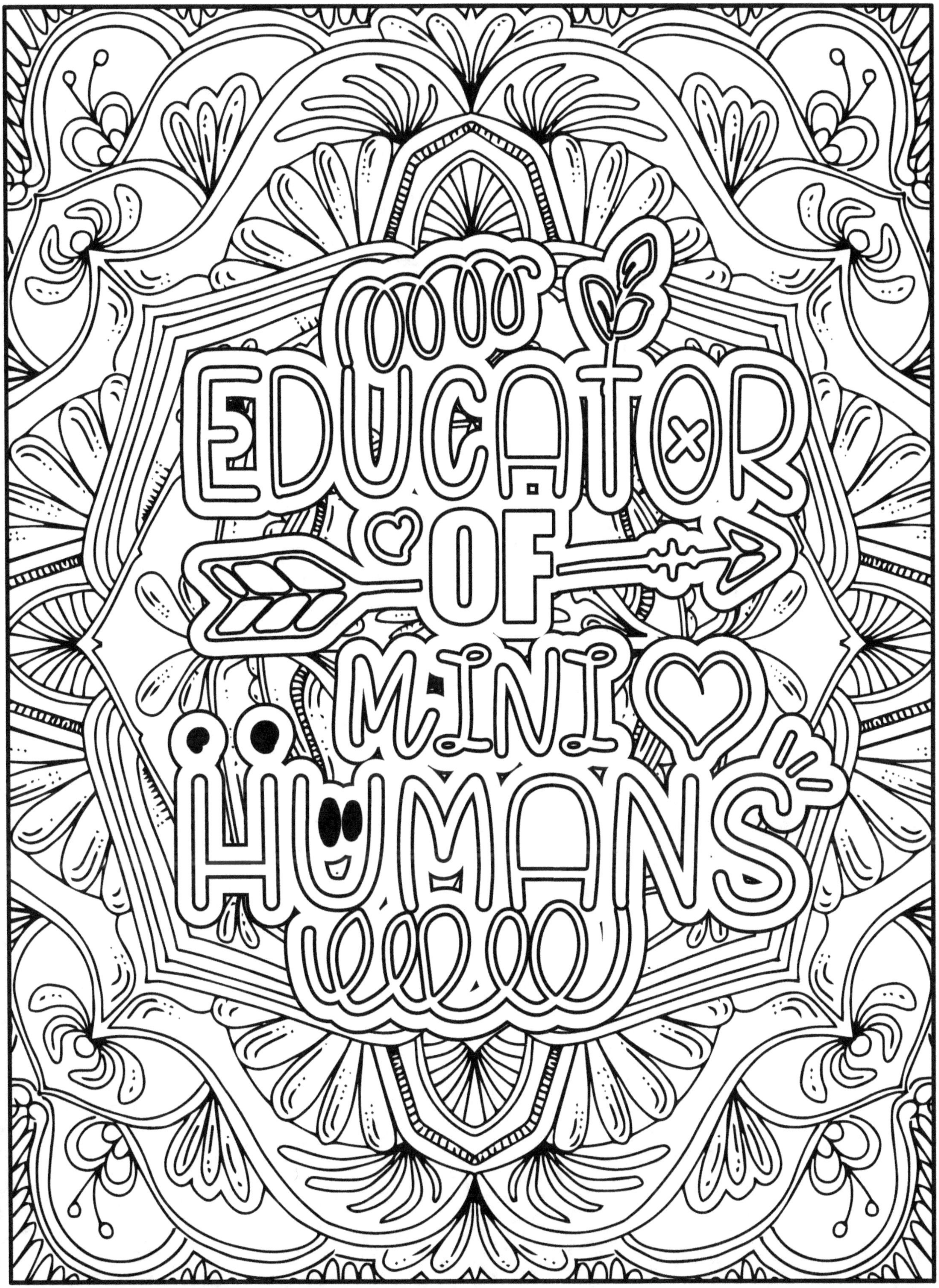
EDUCATOR
OF
MINI
HUMANS

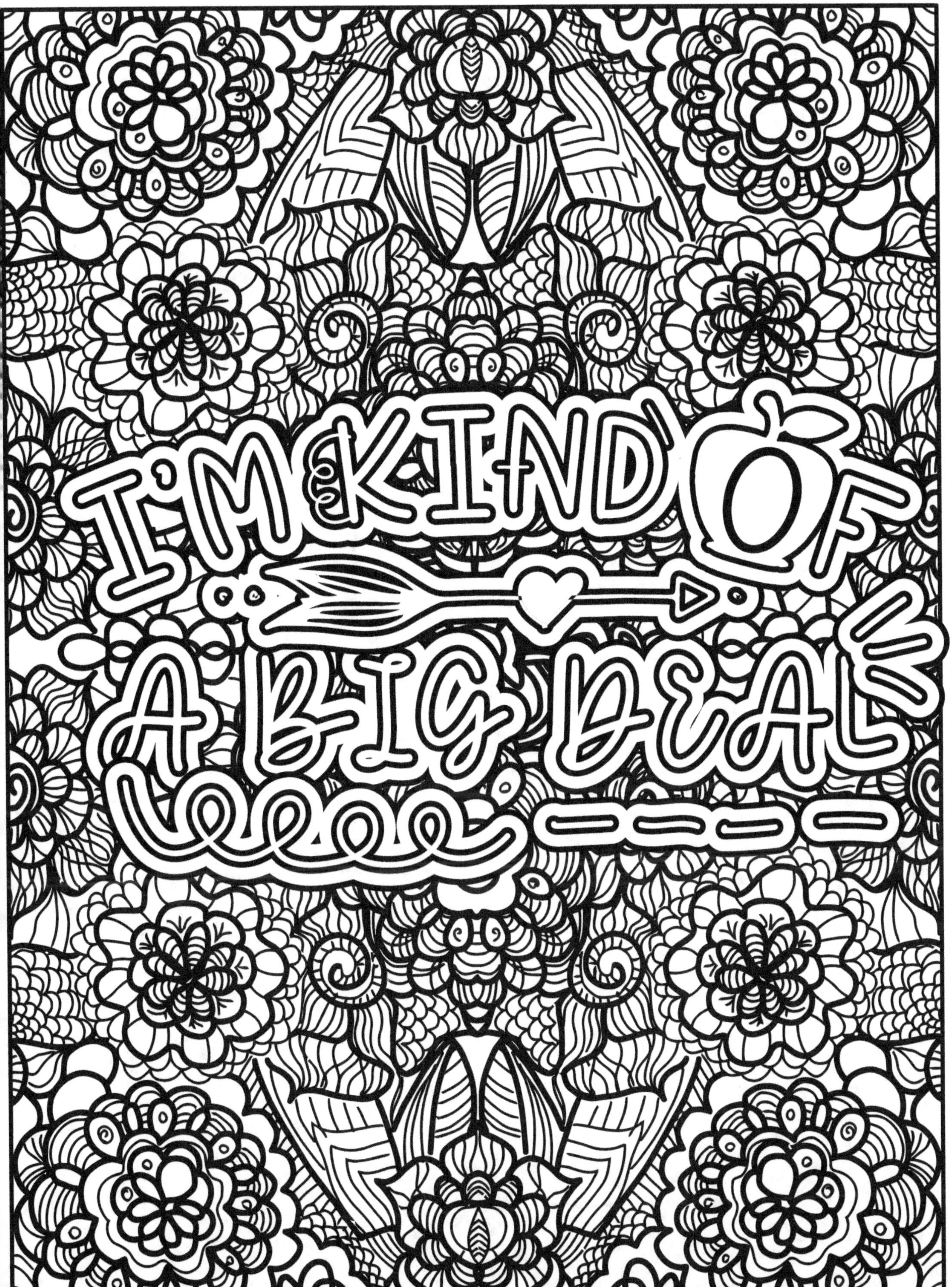
I'M KIND OF
A BIG DEAL

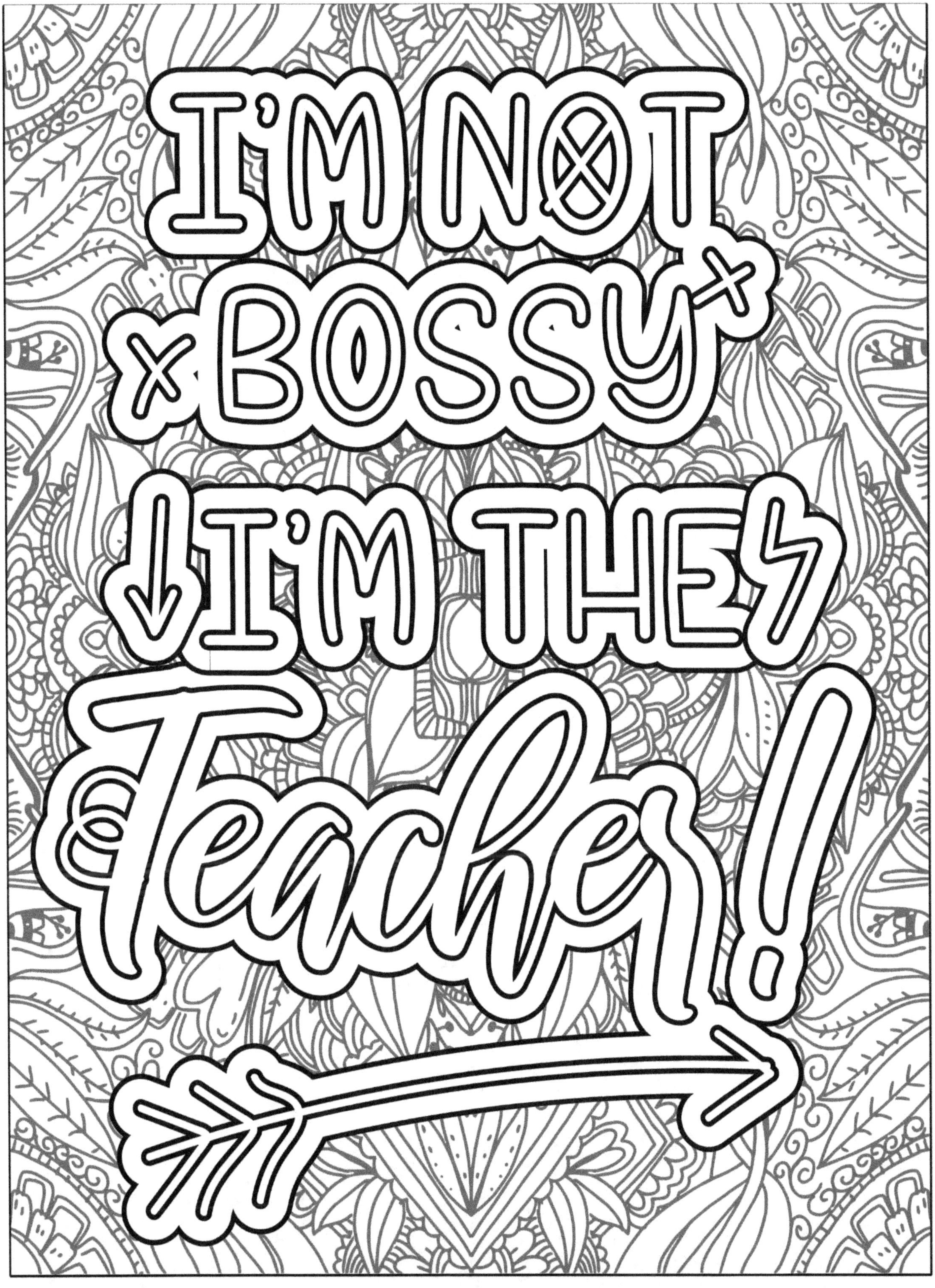
I'M NOT
BOSSY
I'M THE
Teacher!

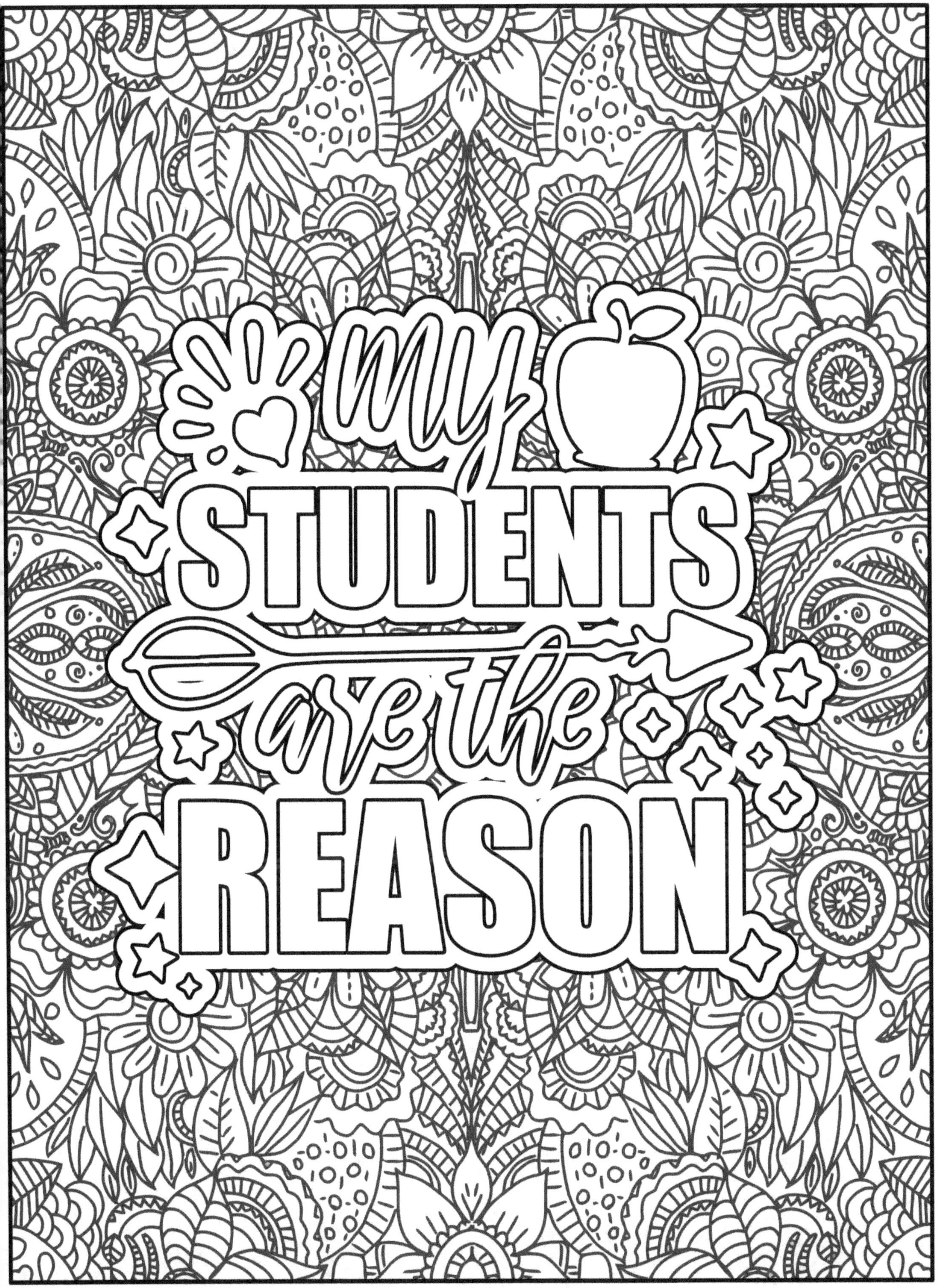
my
STUDENTS
are the
REASON

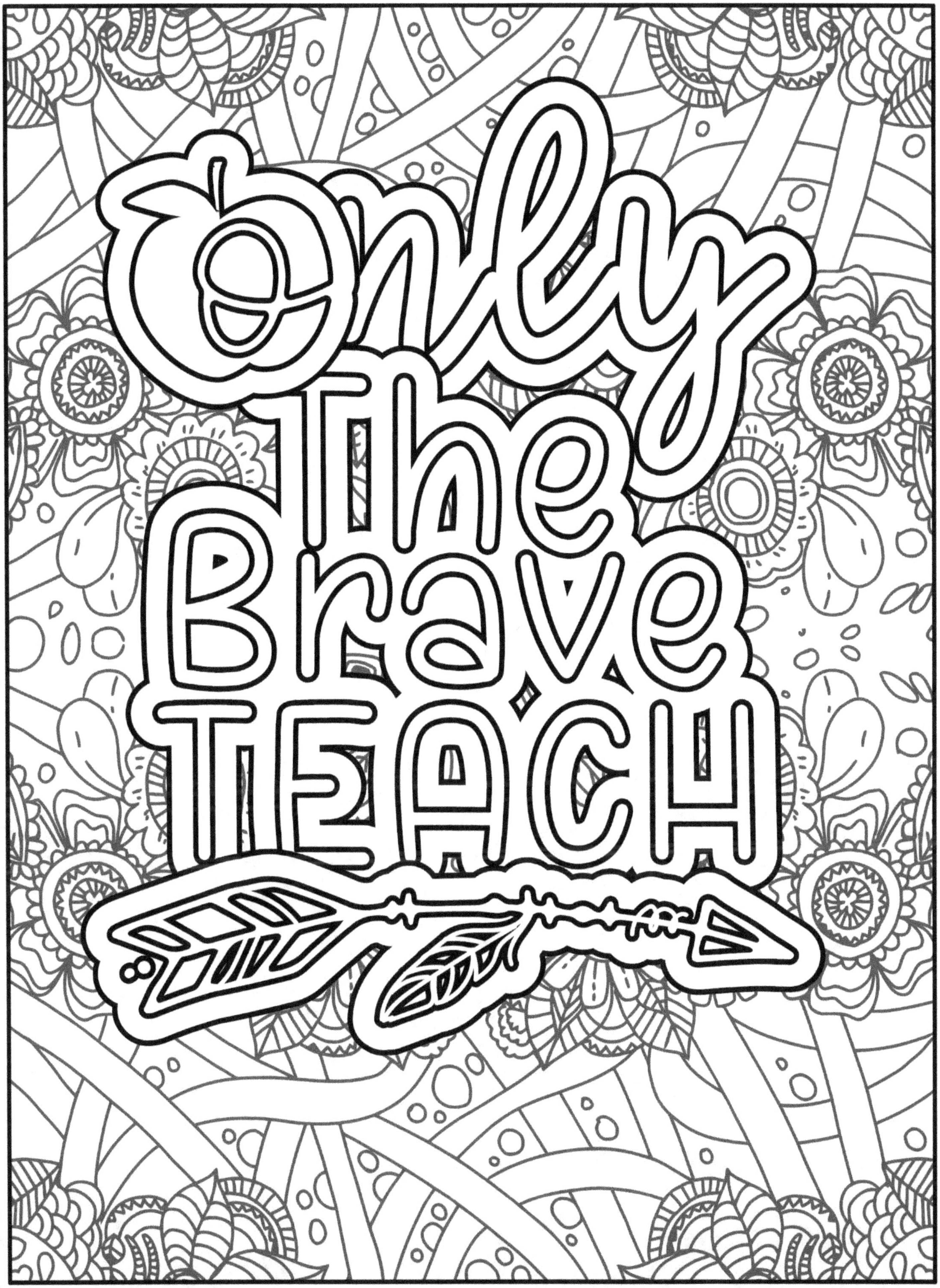
Only
The
Brave
TEACH

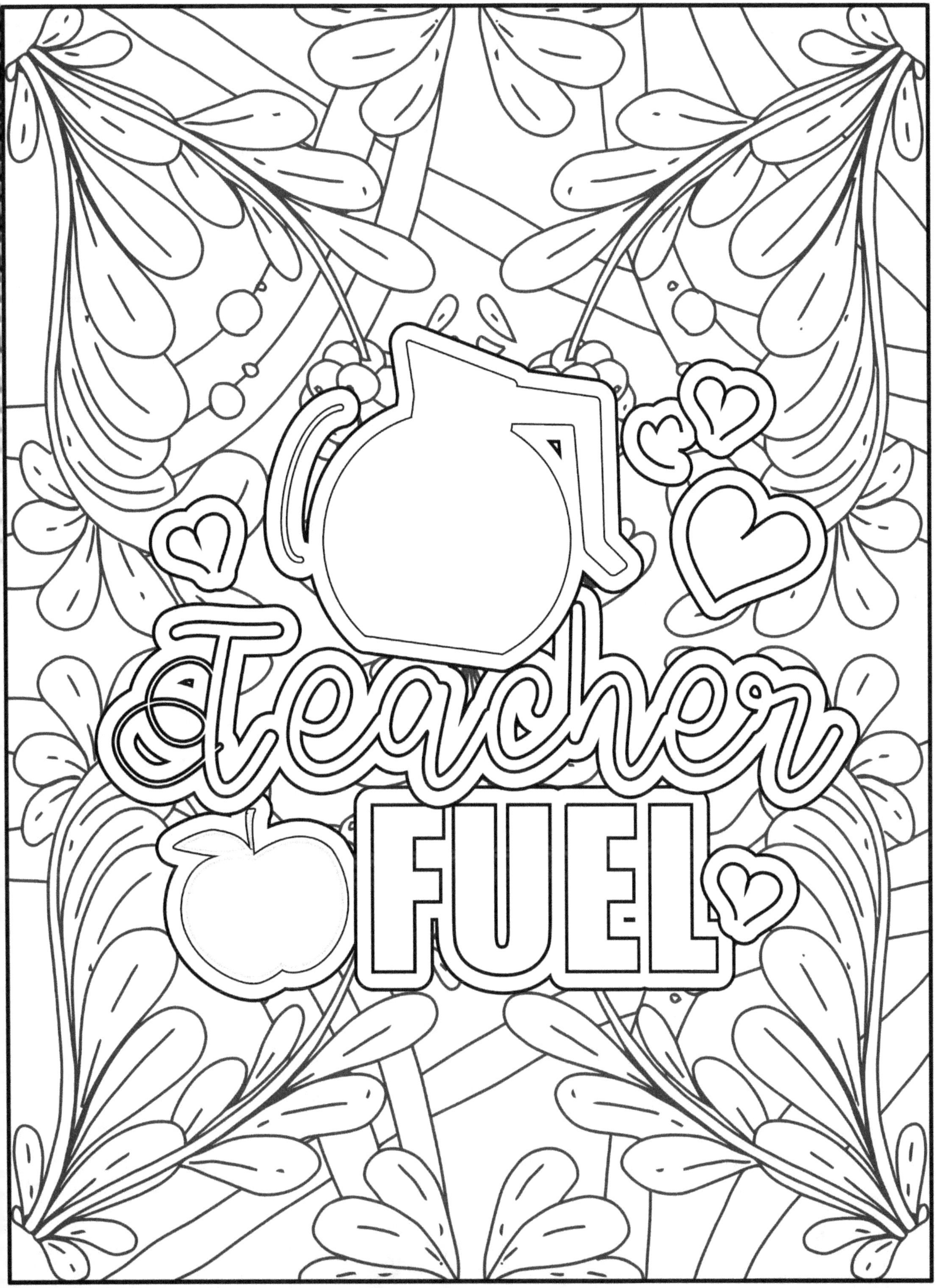
Teacher
FUEL

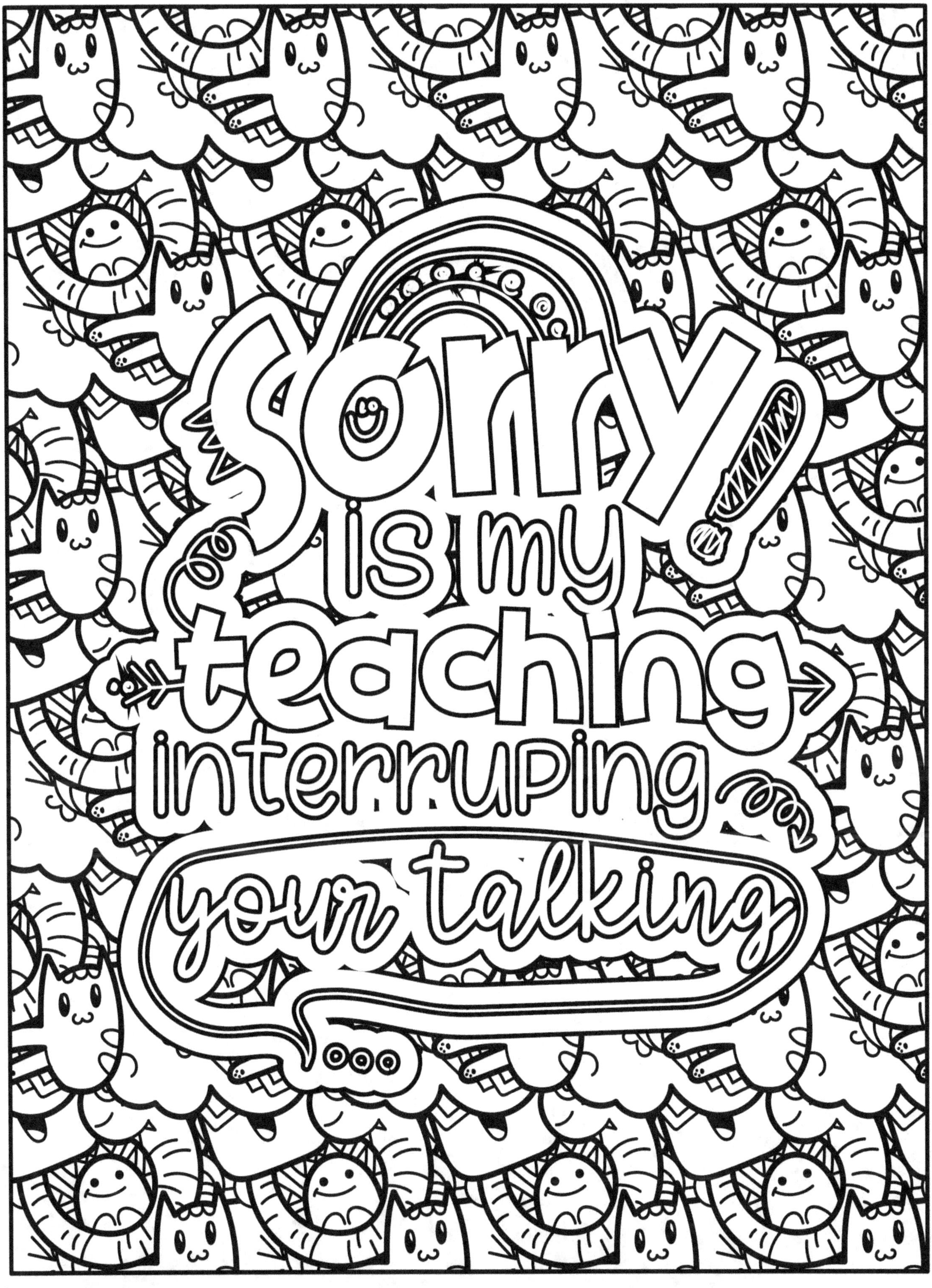
Sorry!
is my
teaching
interruping
your talking

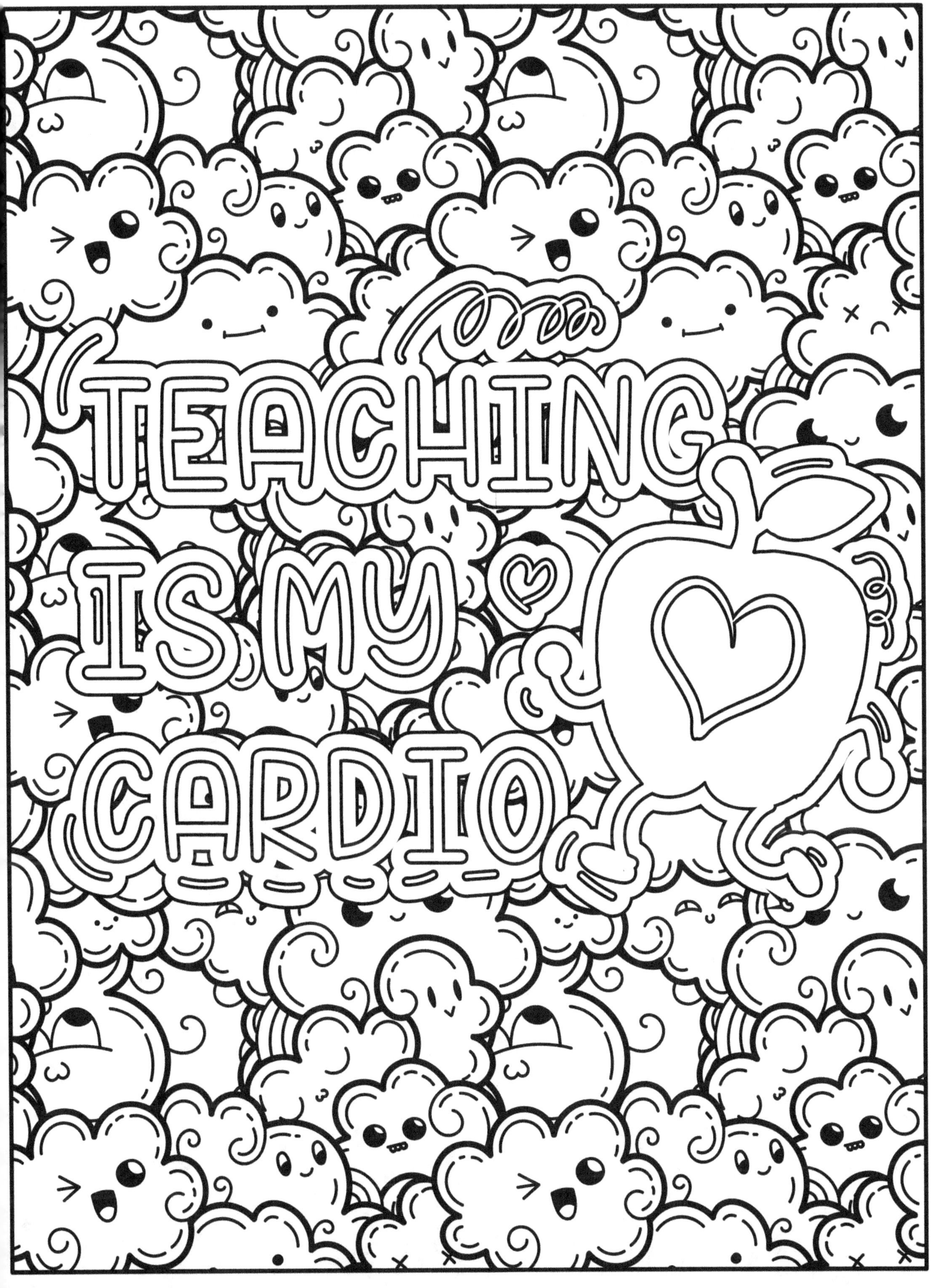
'TEACHING
IS MY
CARDIO

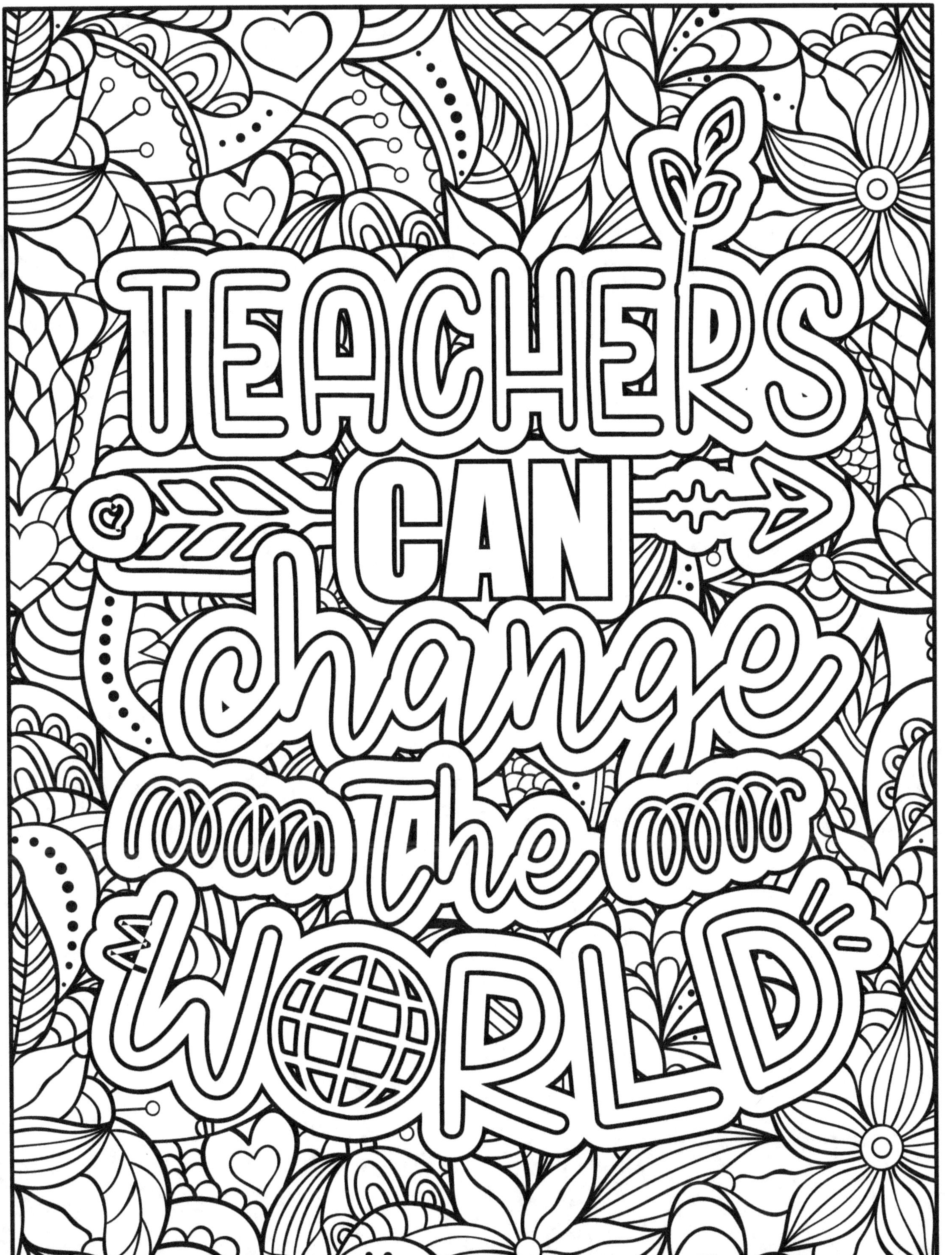
TEACHERS
CAN
change
The
WORLD

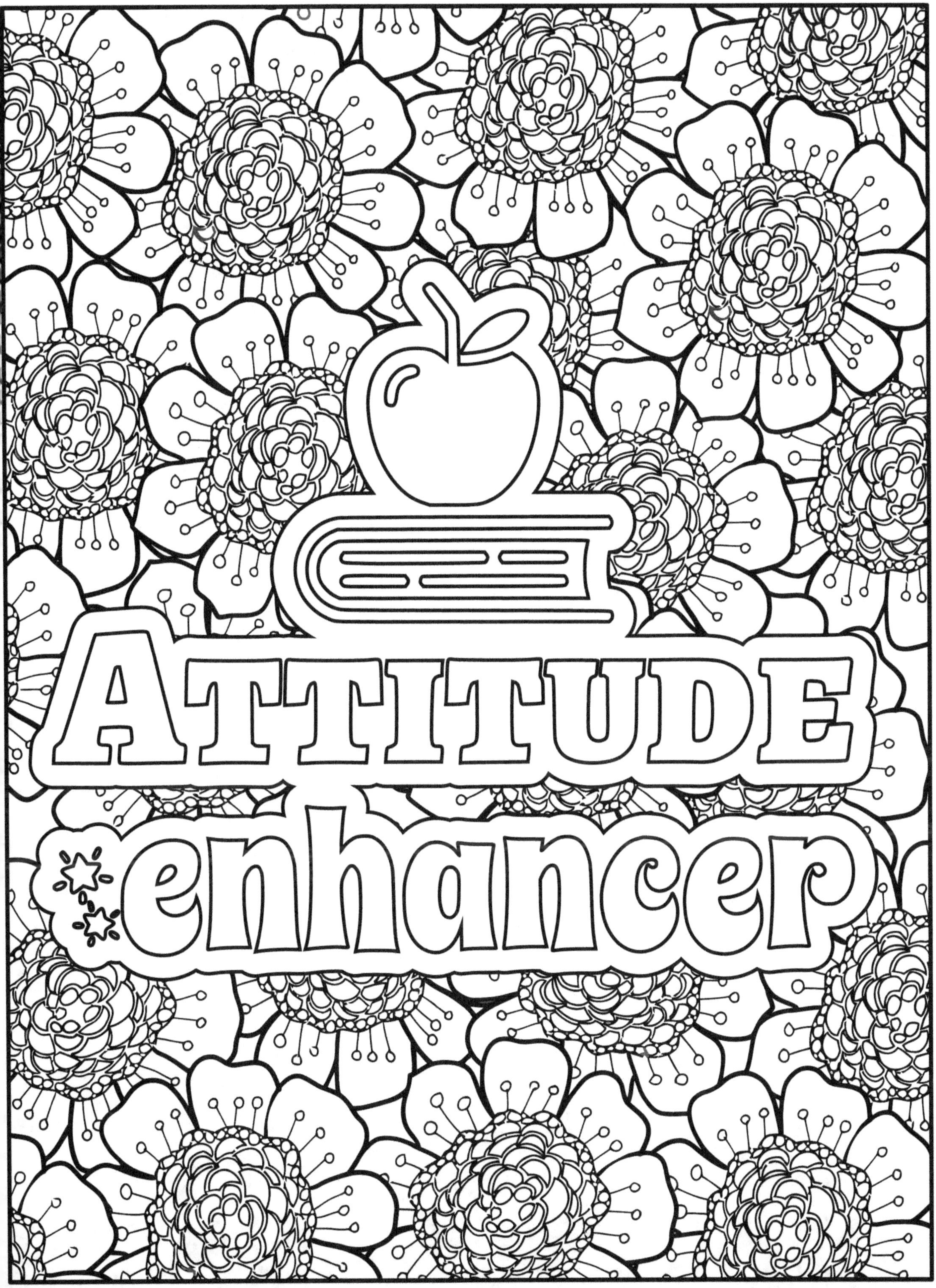
ATTITUDE
enhancer

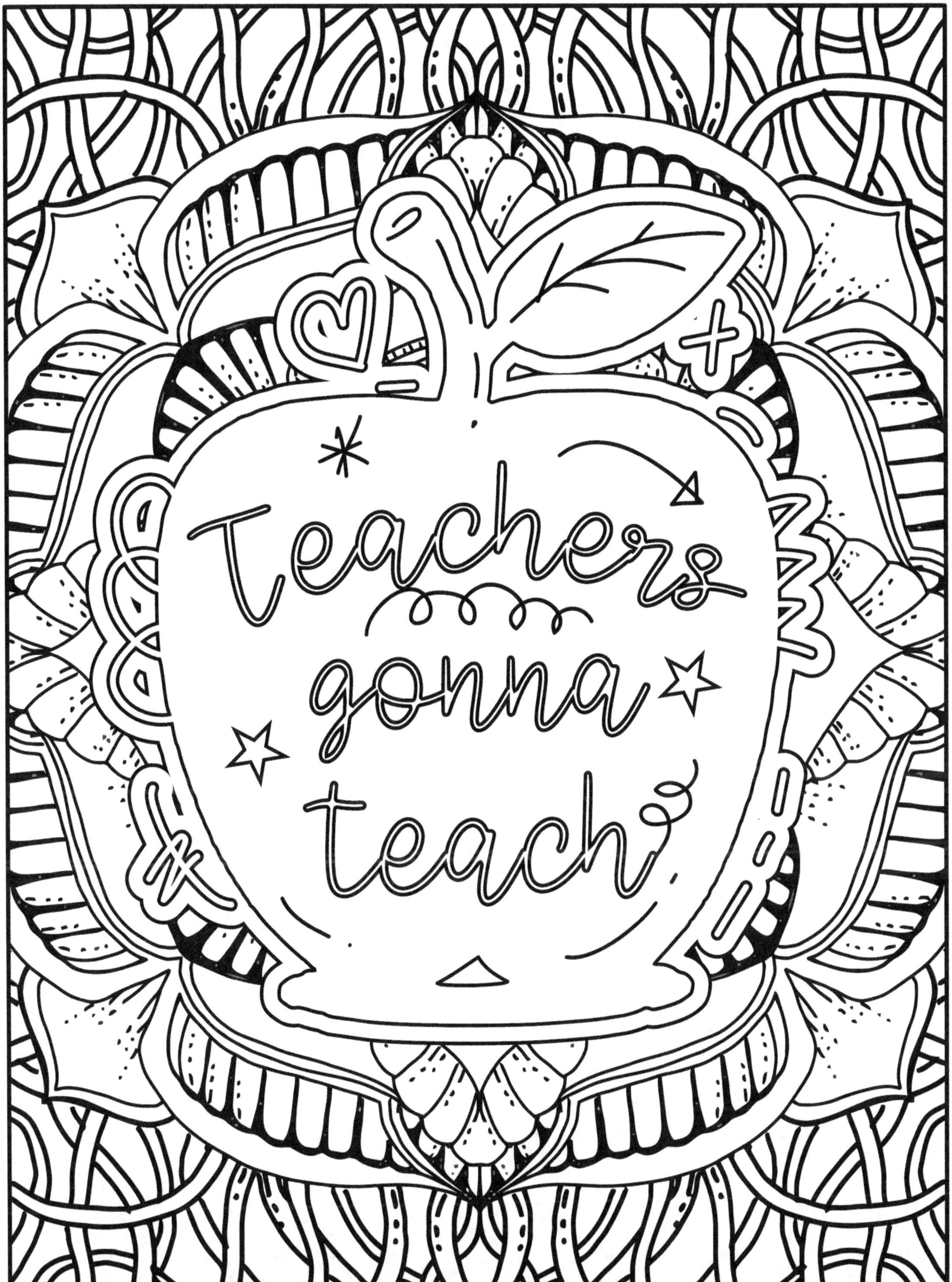
Teachers
gonna
teach

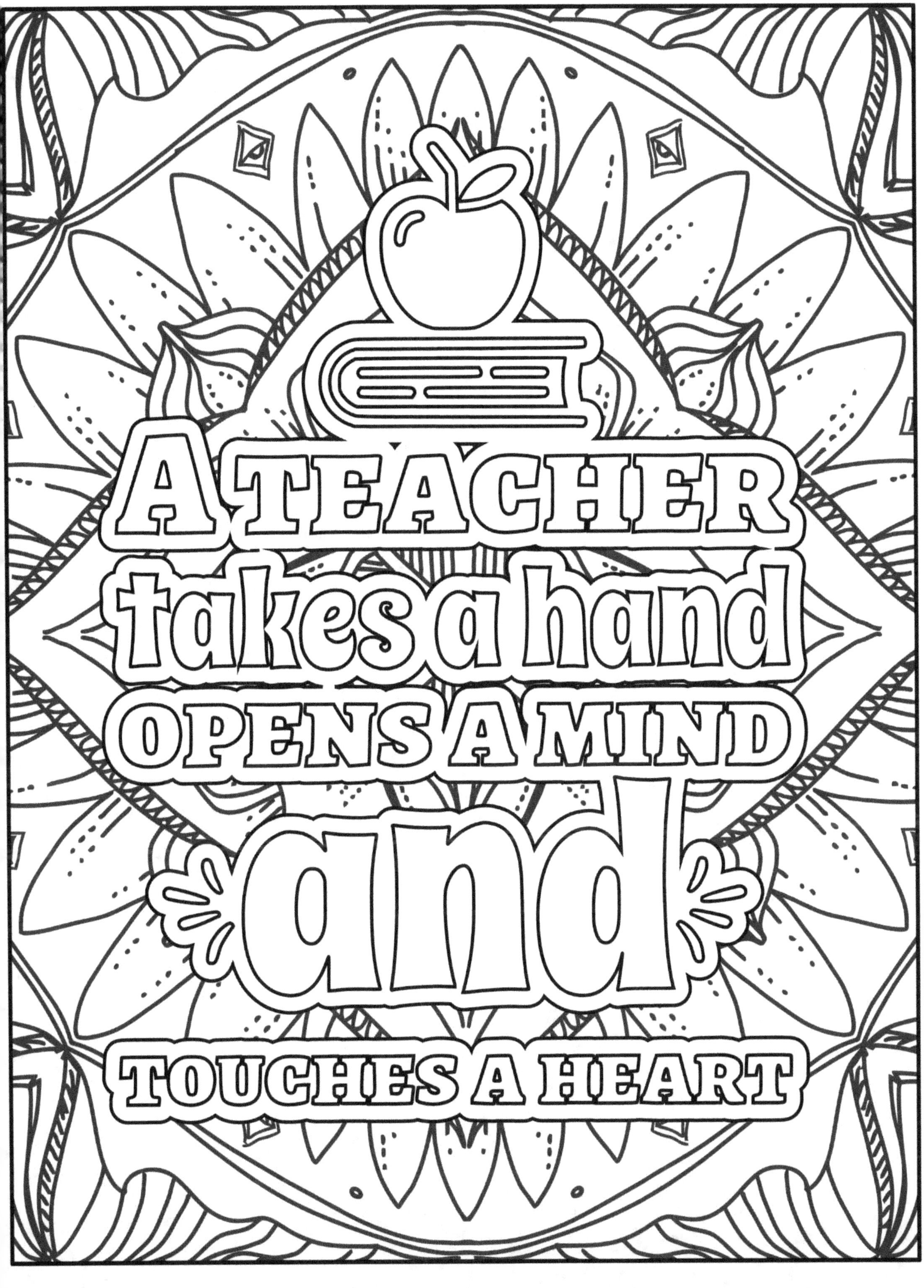
A TEACHER
takes a hand
OPENS A MIND
and
TOUCHES A HEART

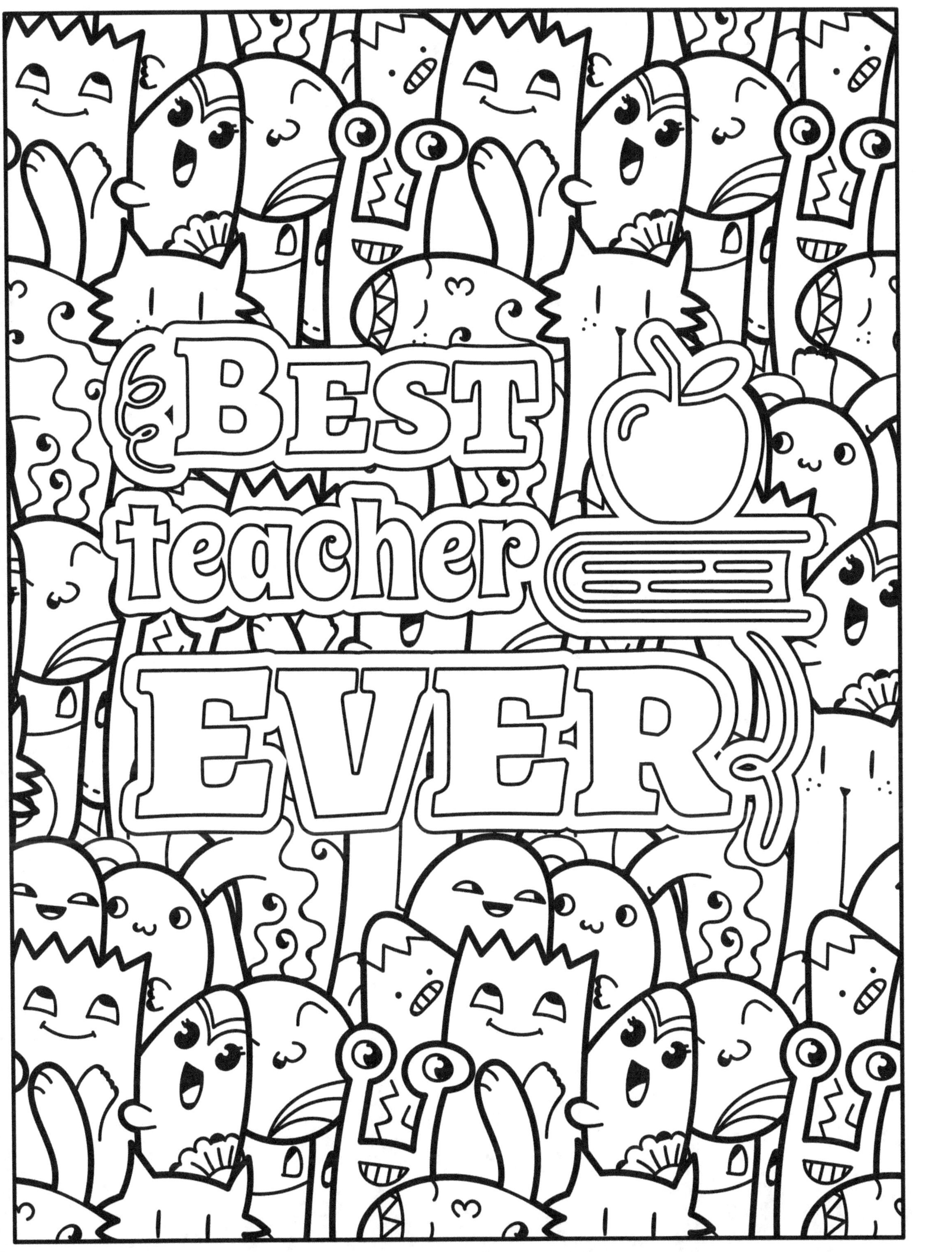
Best teacher EVER

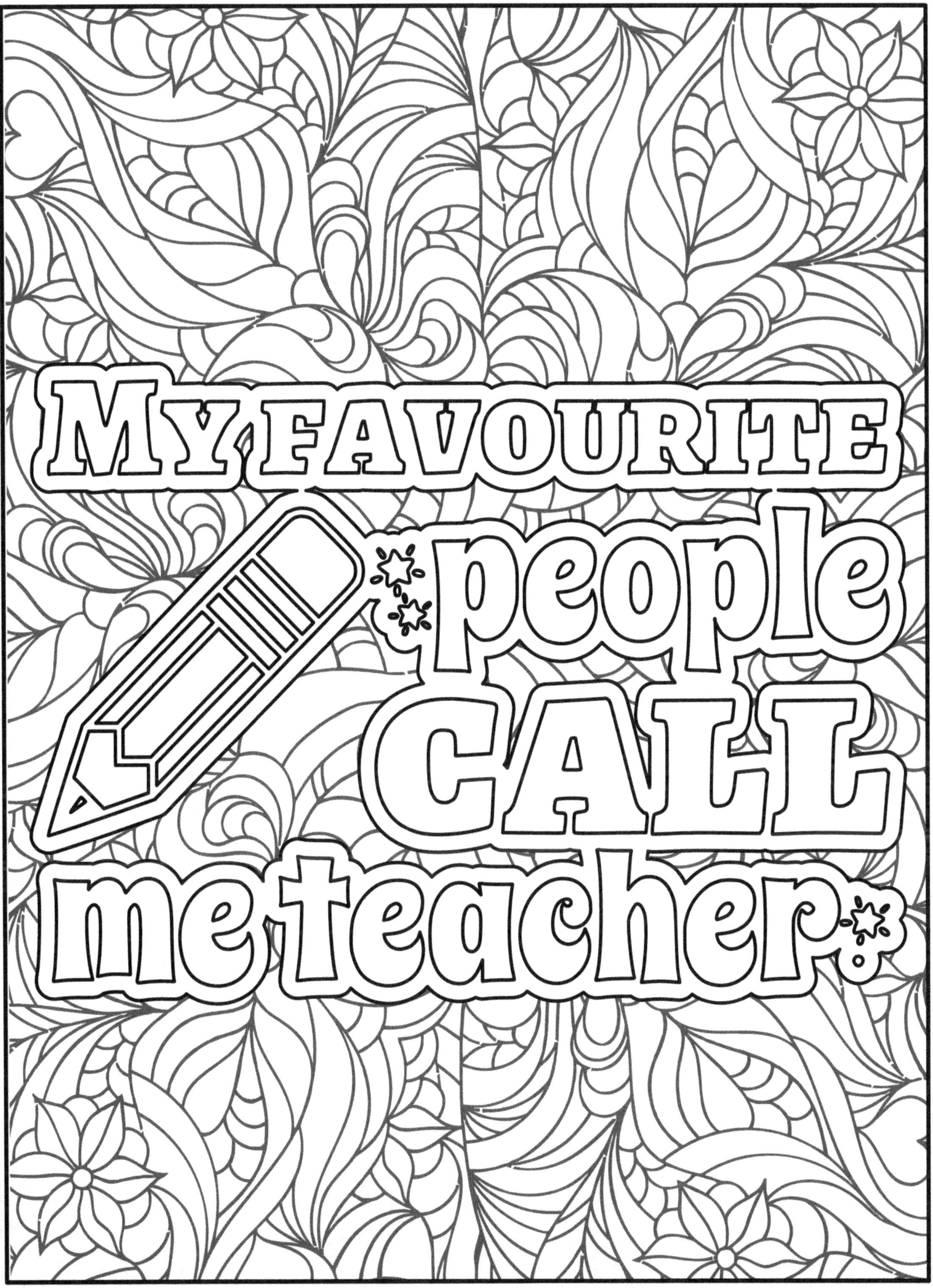
My favourite
people
CALL
me teacher

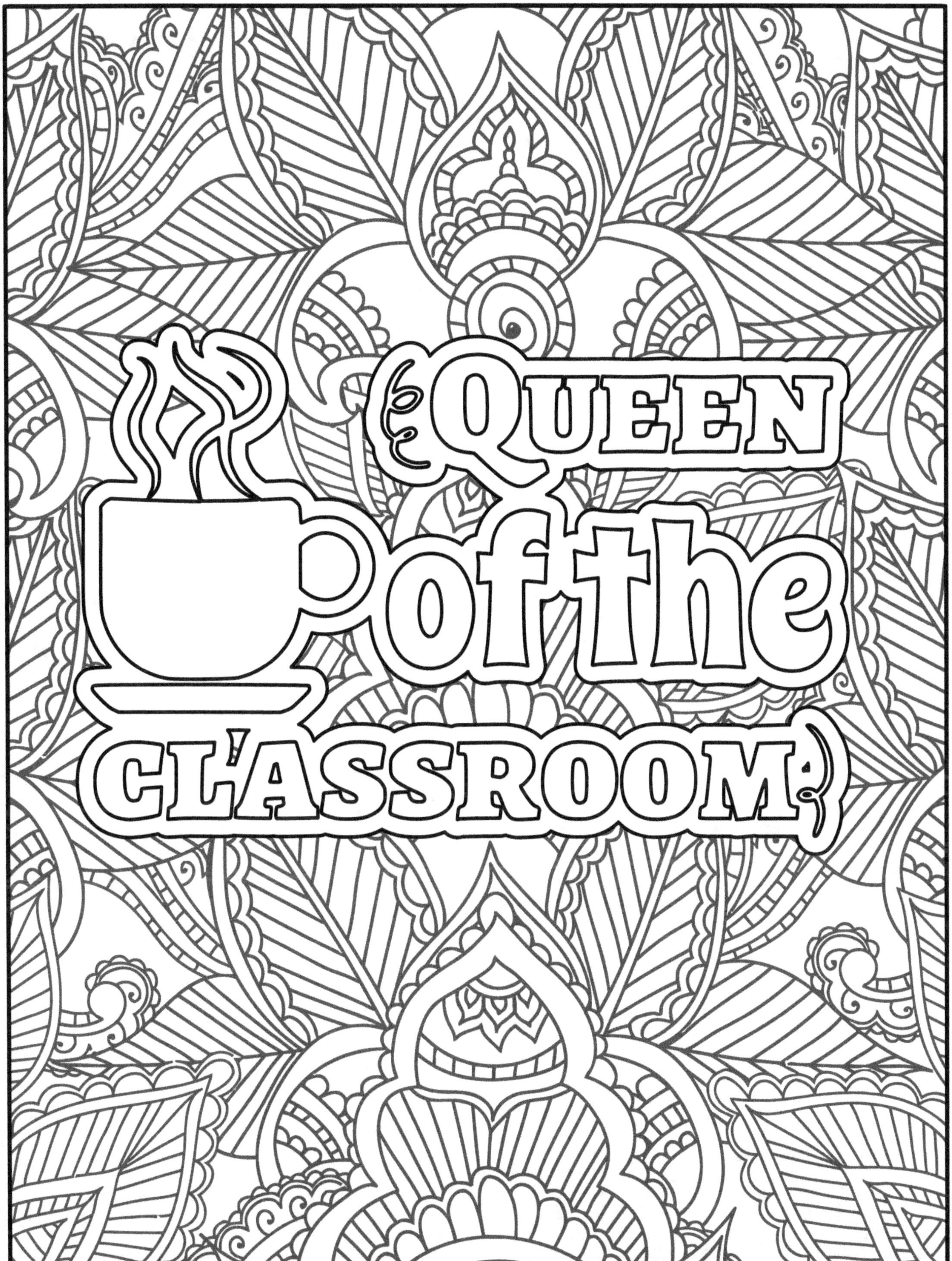
QUEEN
of the
CLASSROOM

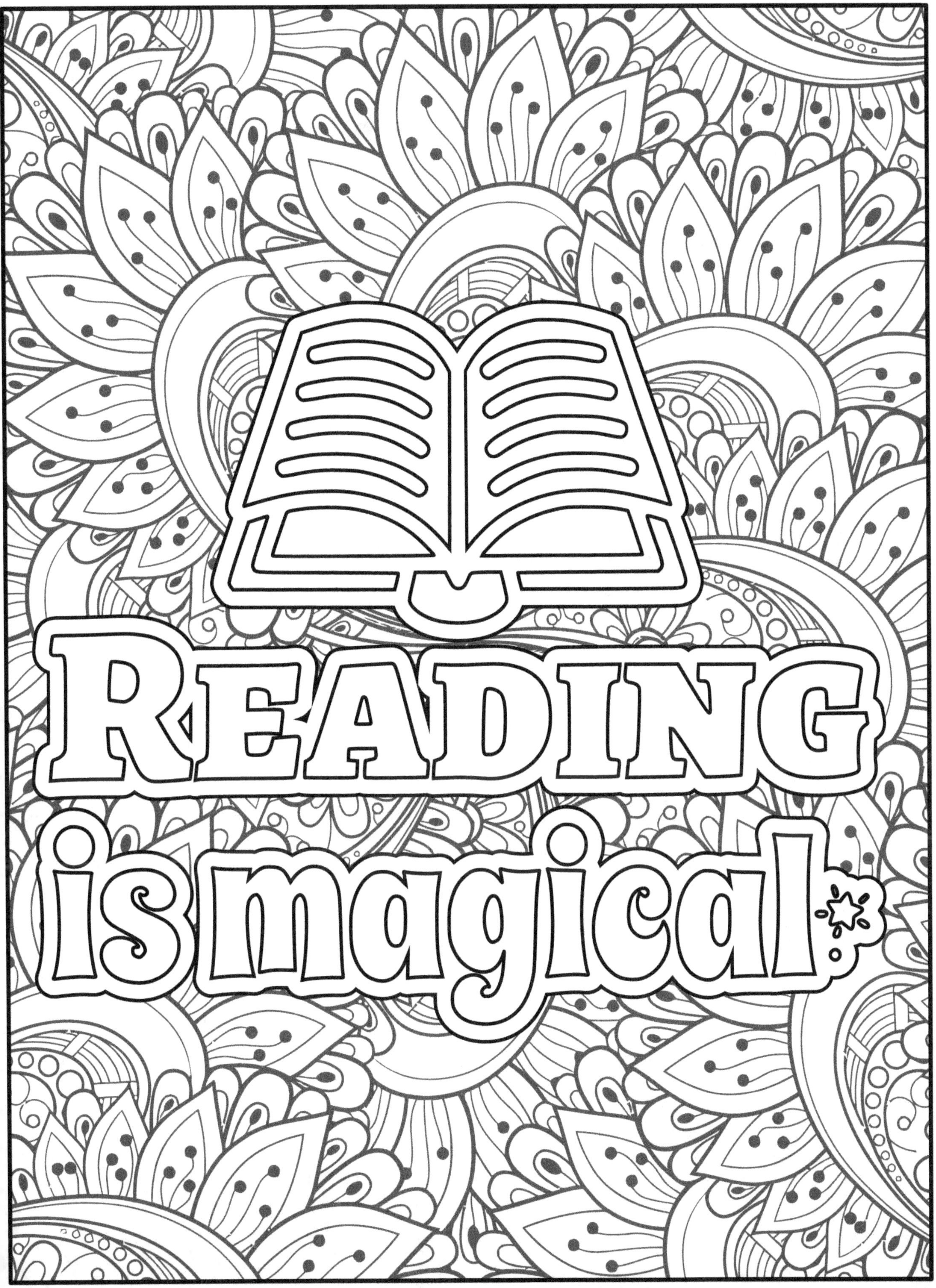
READING
is magical

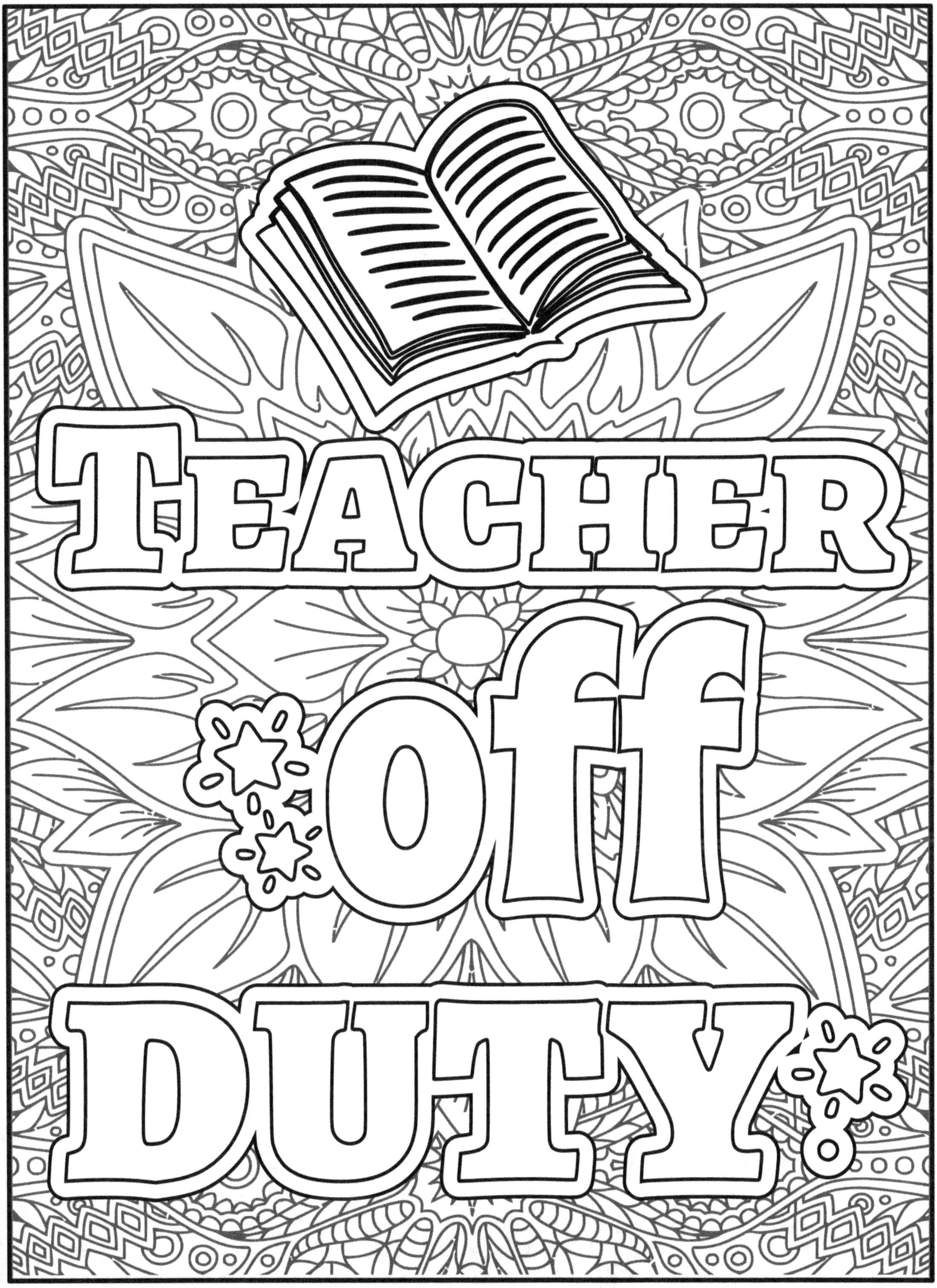
TEACHER
off
DUTY

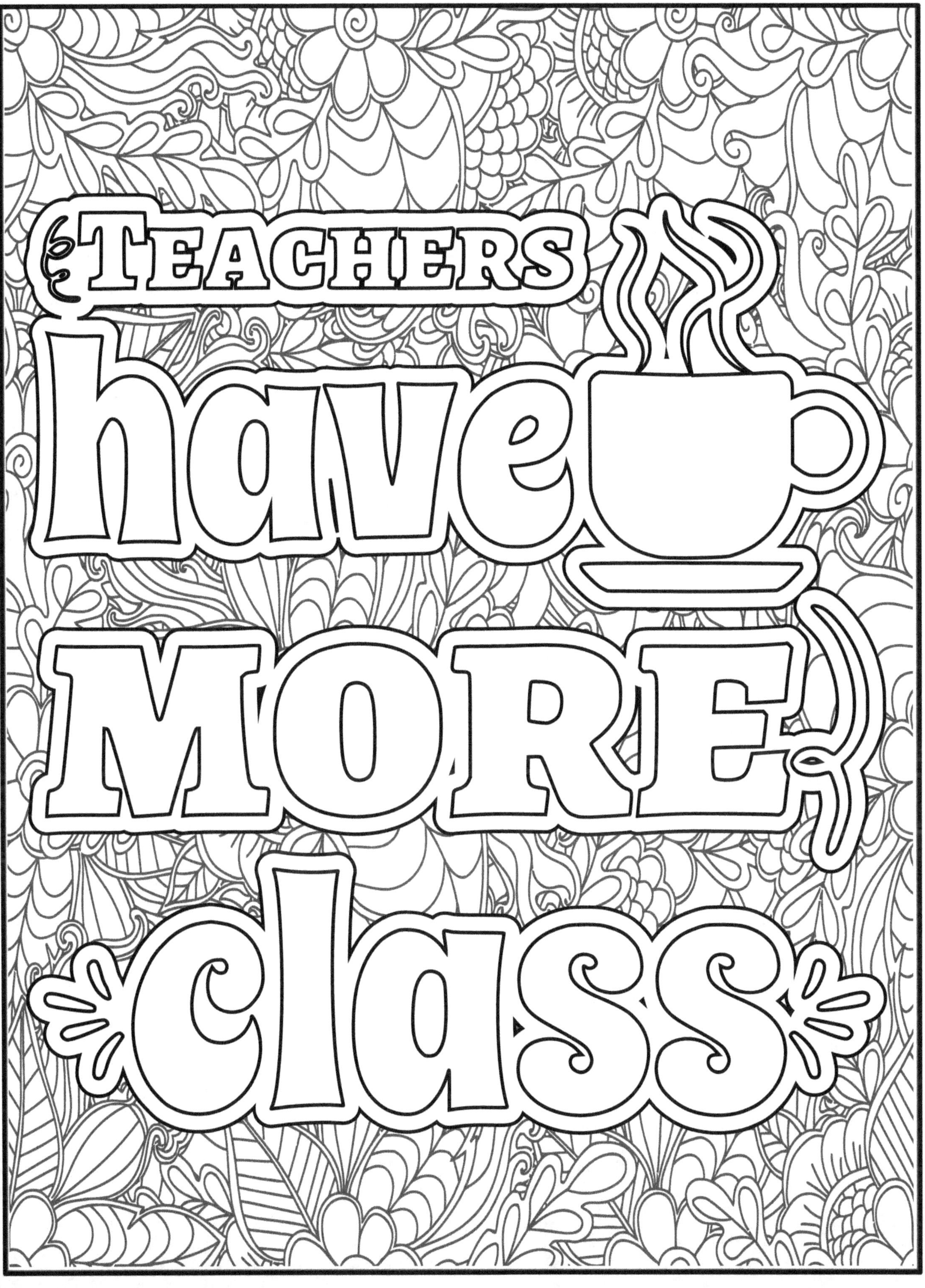
TEACHERS
have
MORE
class

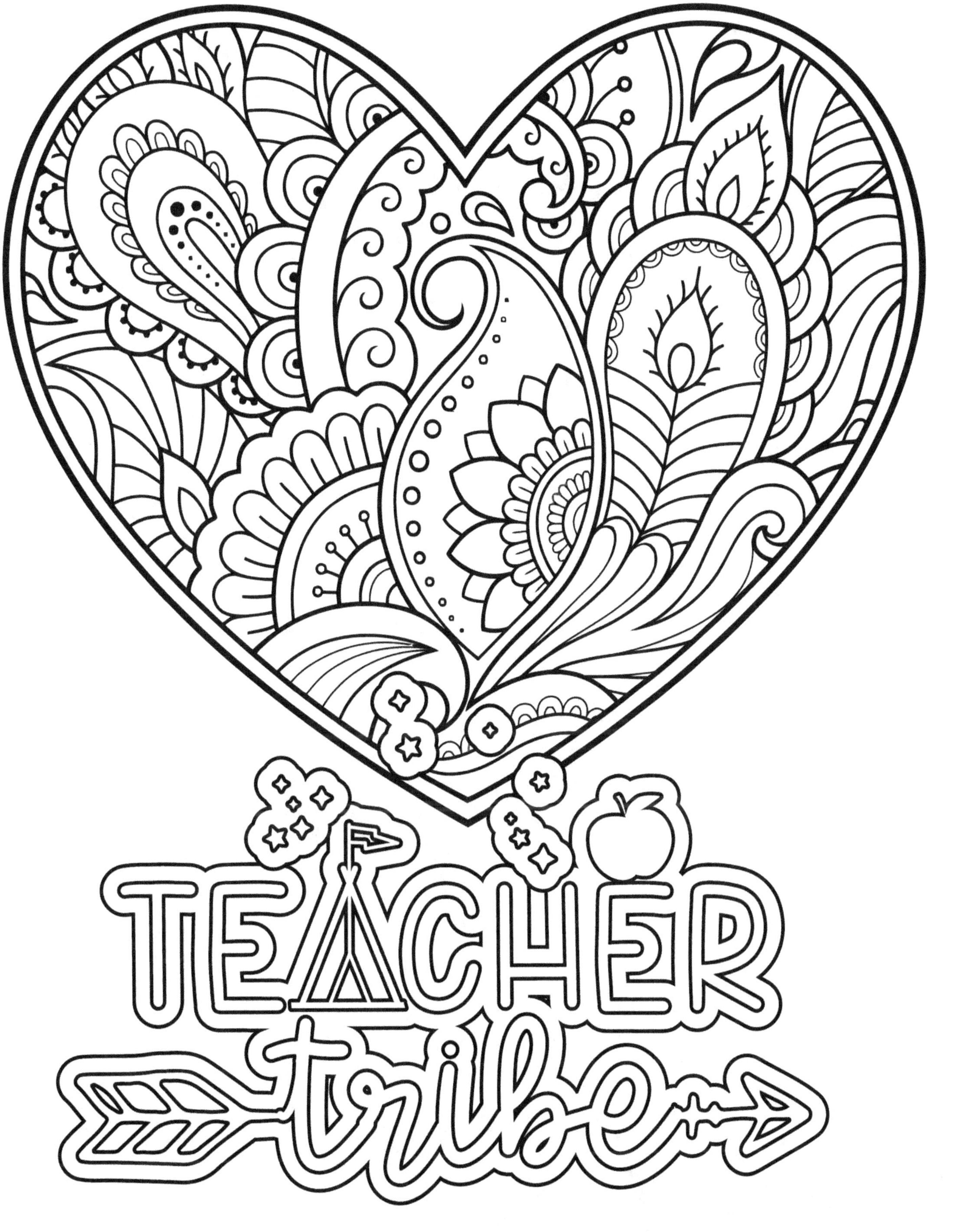
TEACHER
tribe

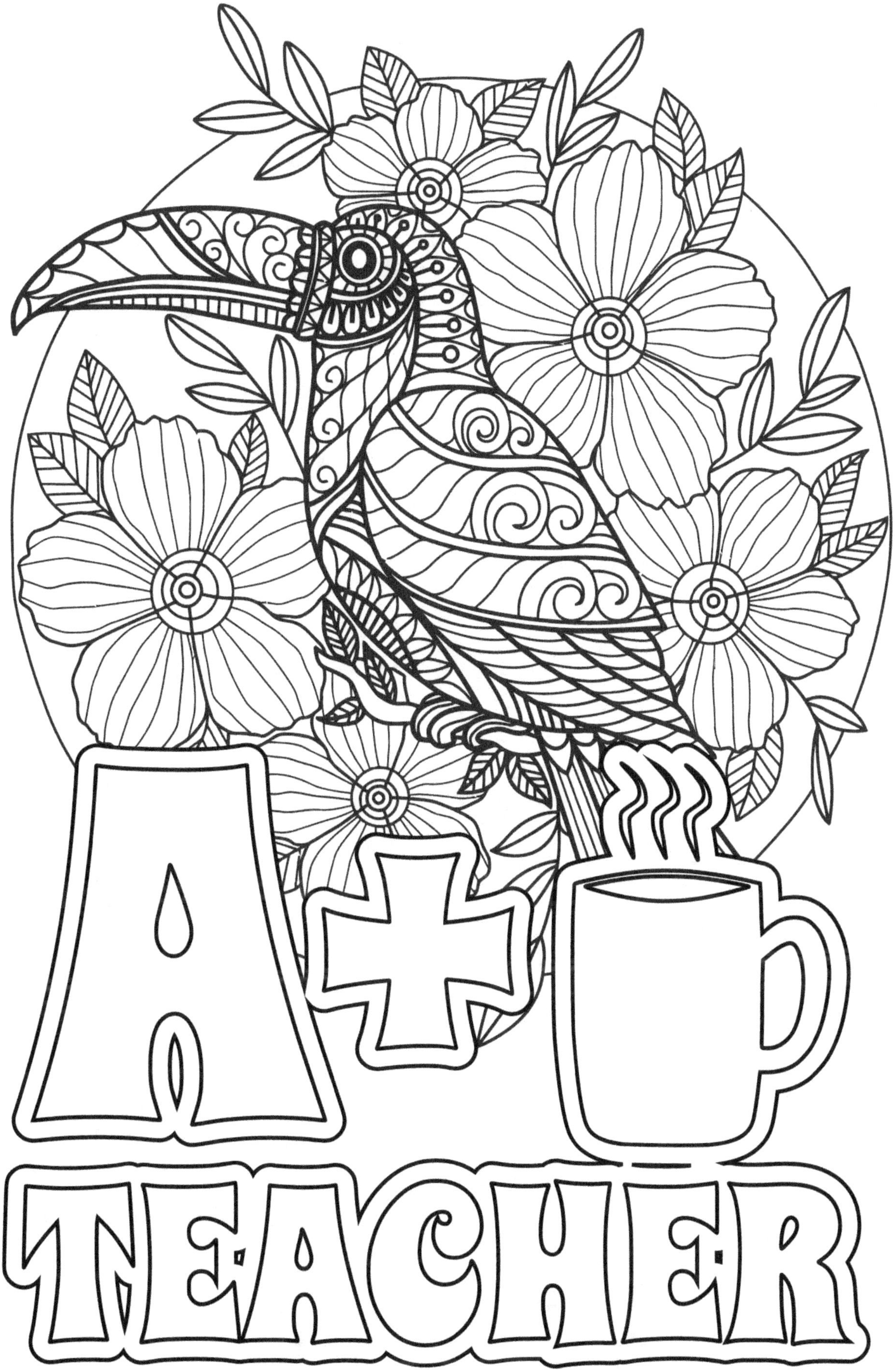
A+
TEACHER

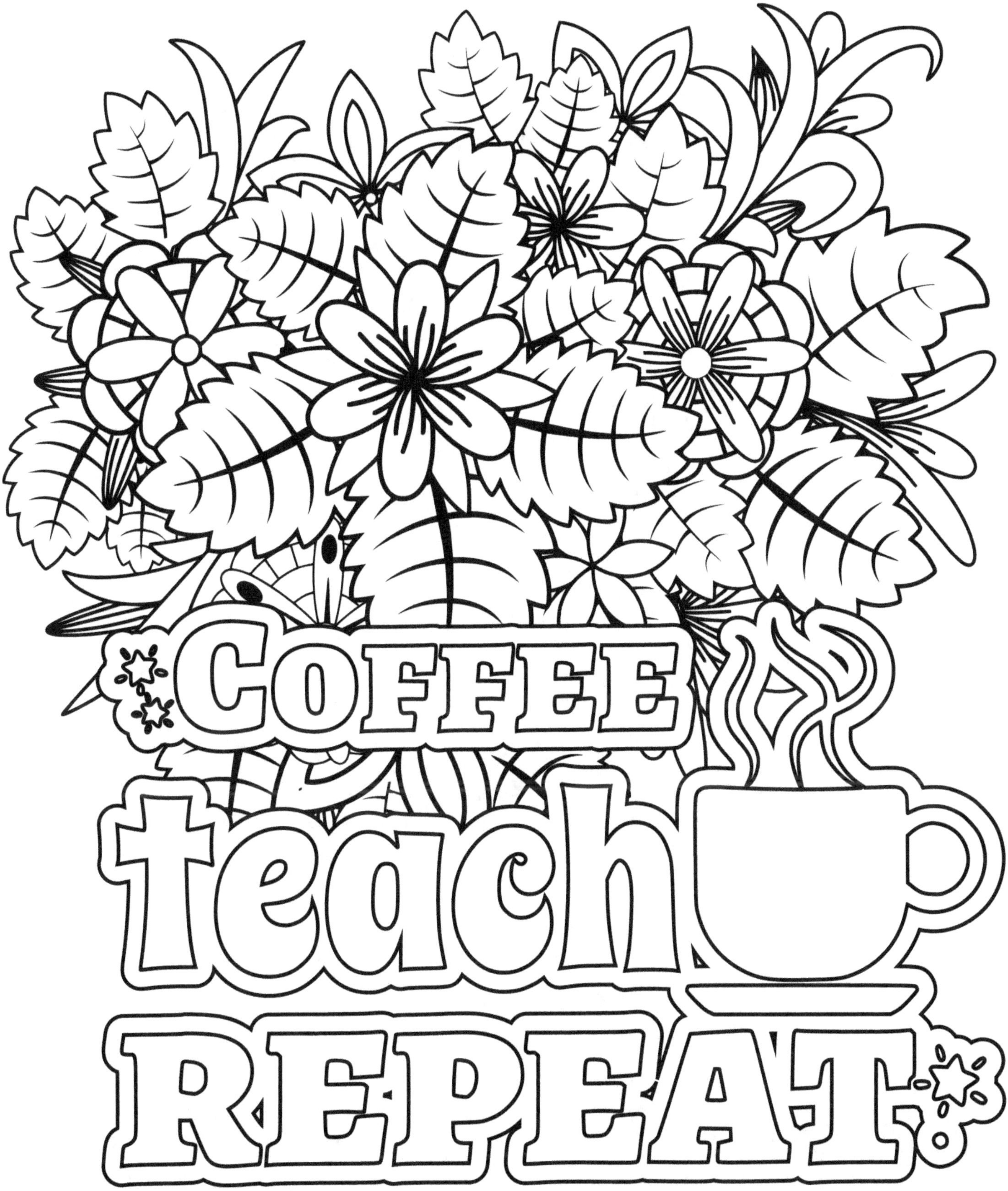
COFFEE
teach
REPEAT

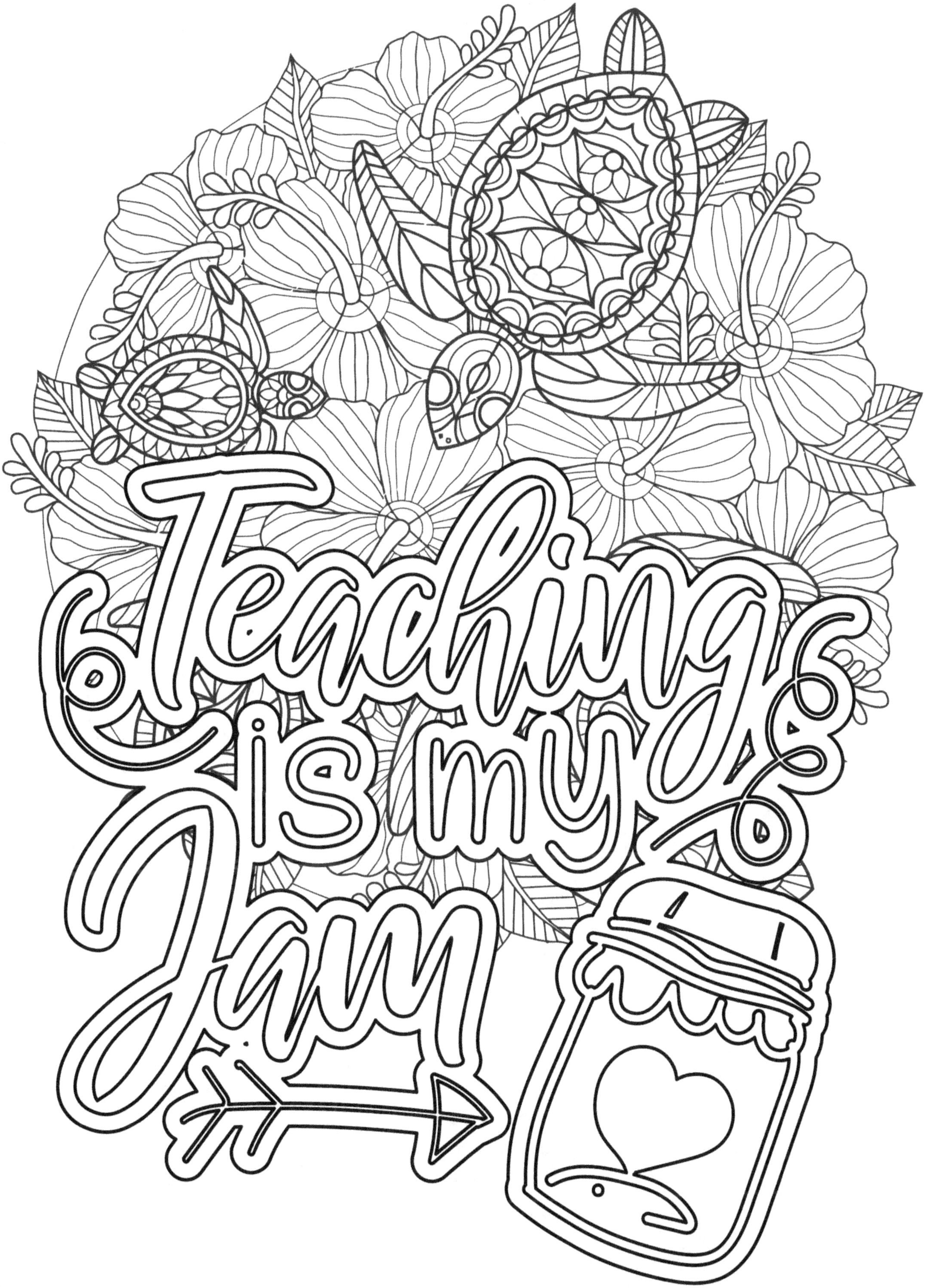
Teaching is my Jam

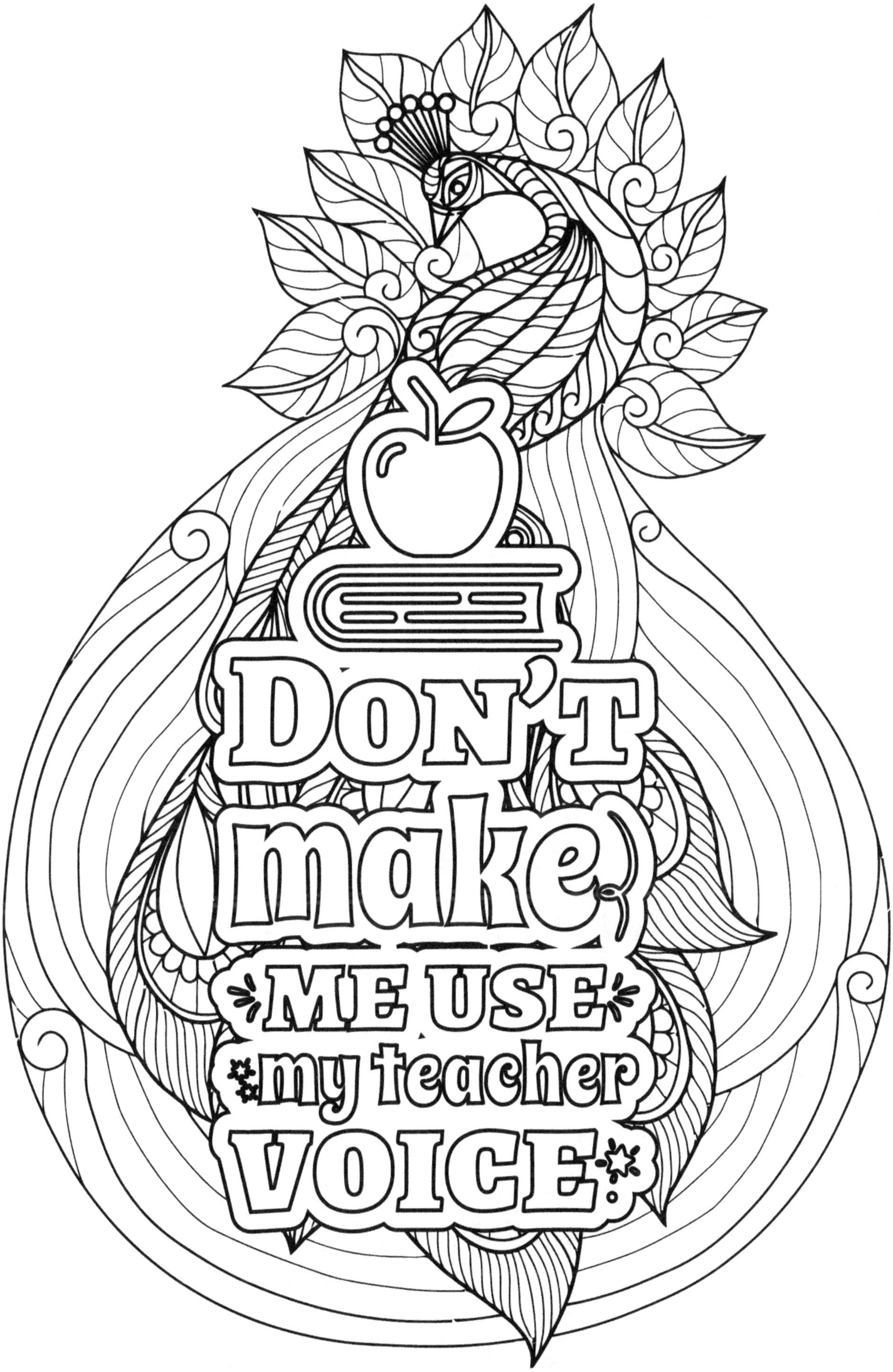
Don't
make
ME USE
my teacher
VOICE

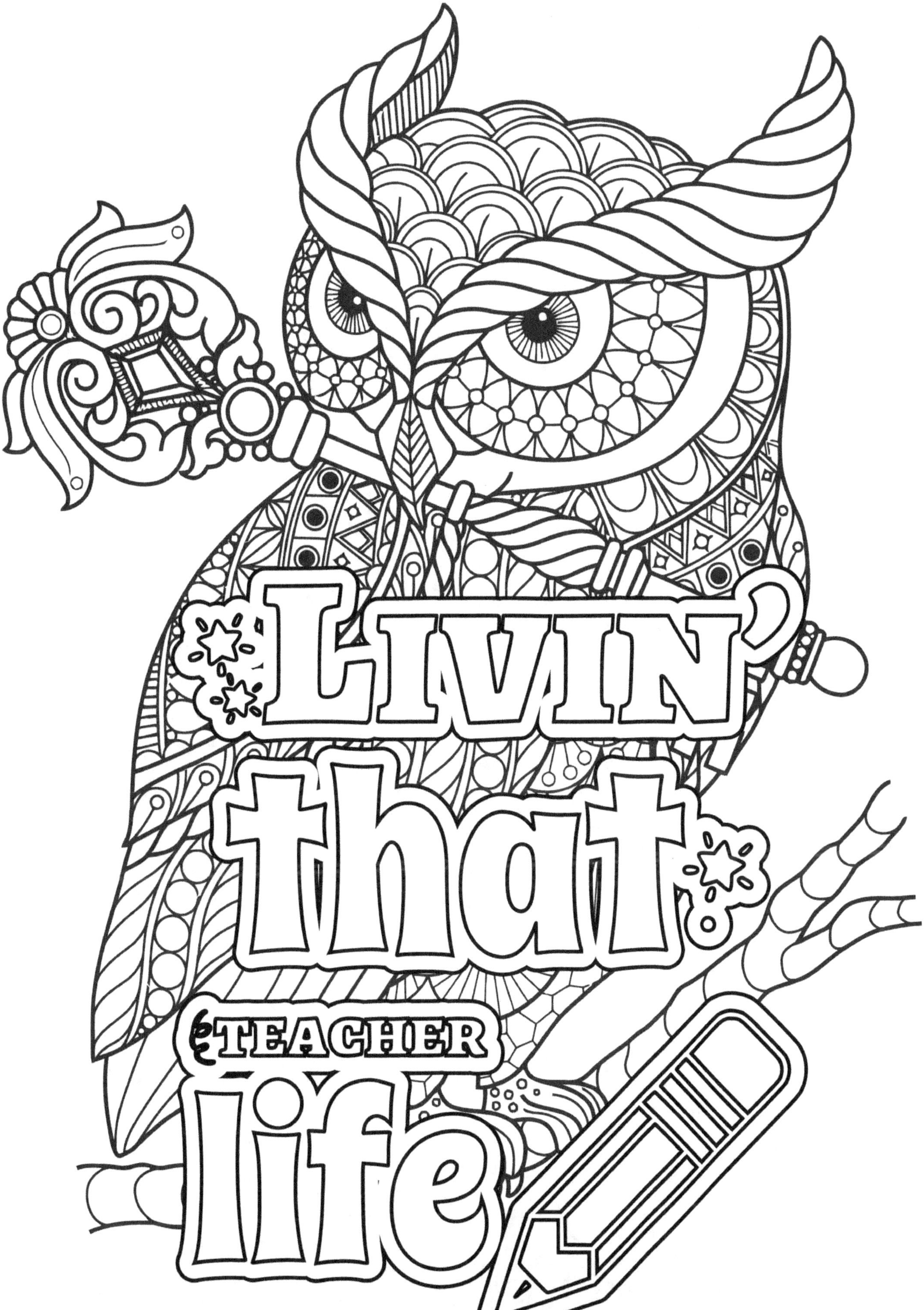
Livin'
that
TEACHER
life

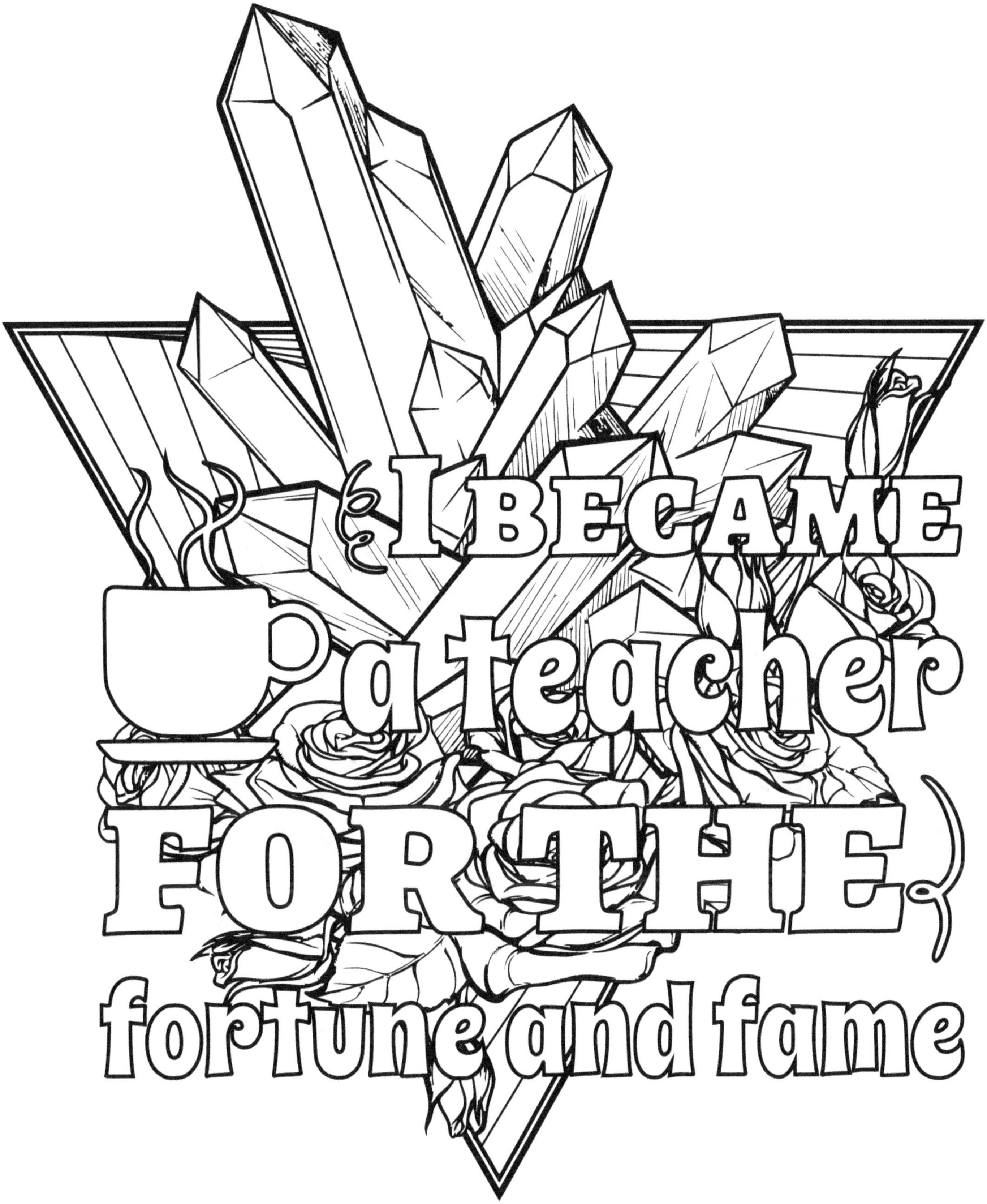
I BECAME
a teacher
FOR THE
fortune and fame

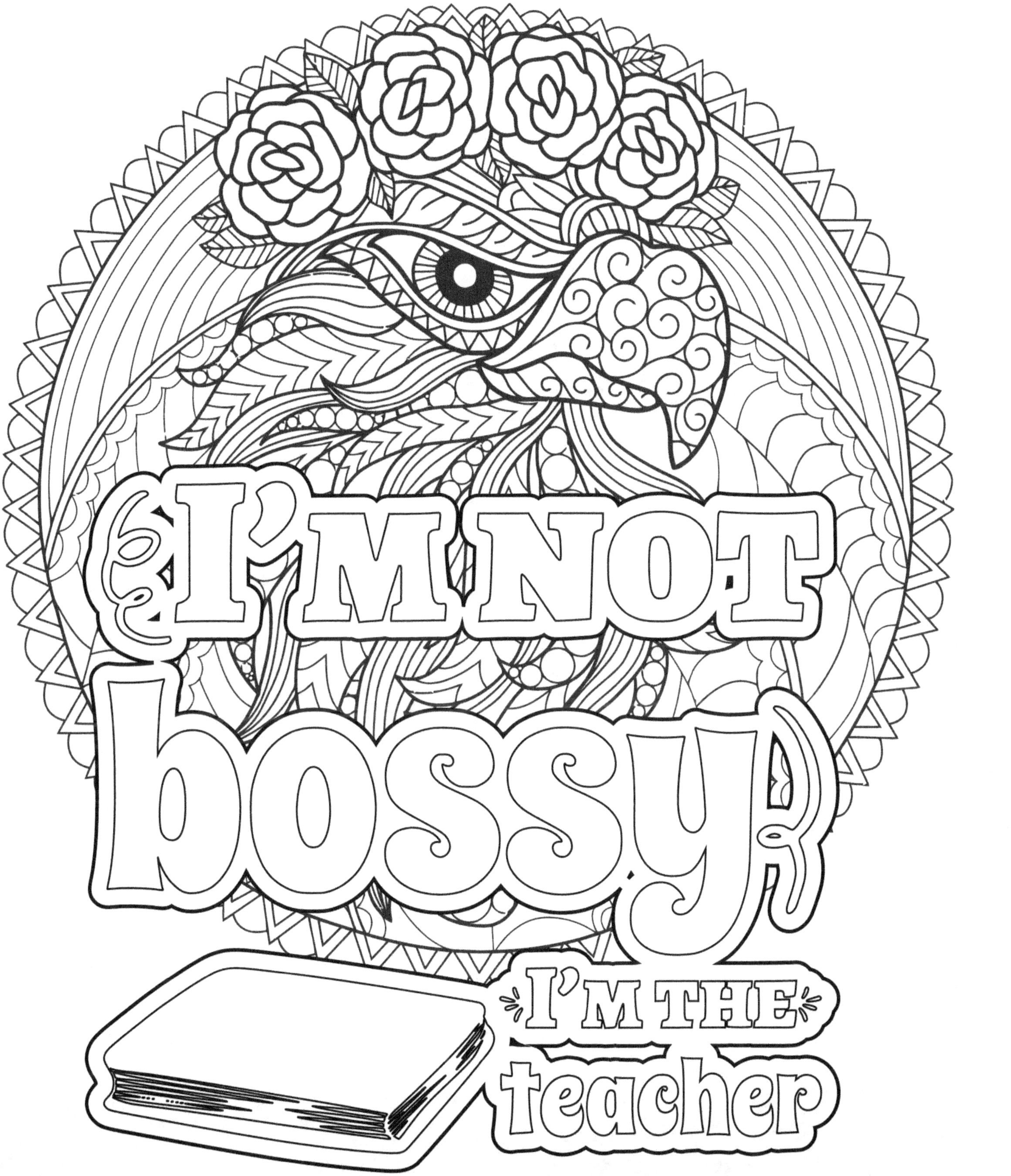
I'M NOT
bossy
I'M THE
teacher

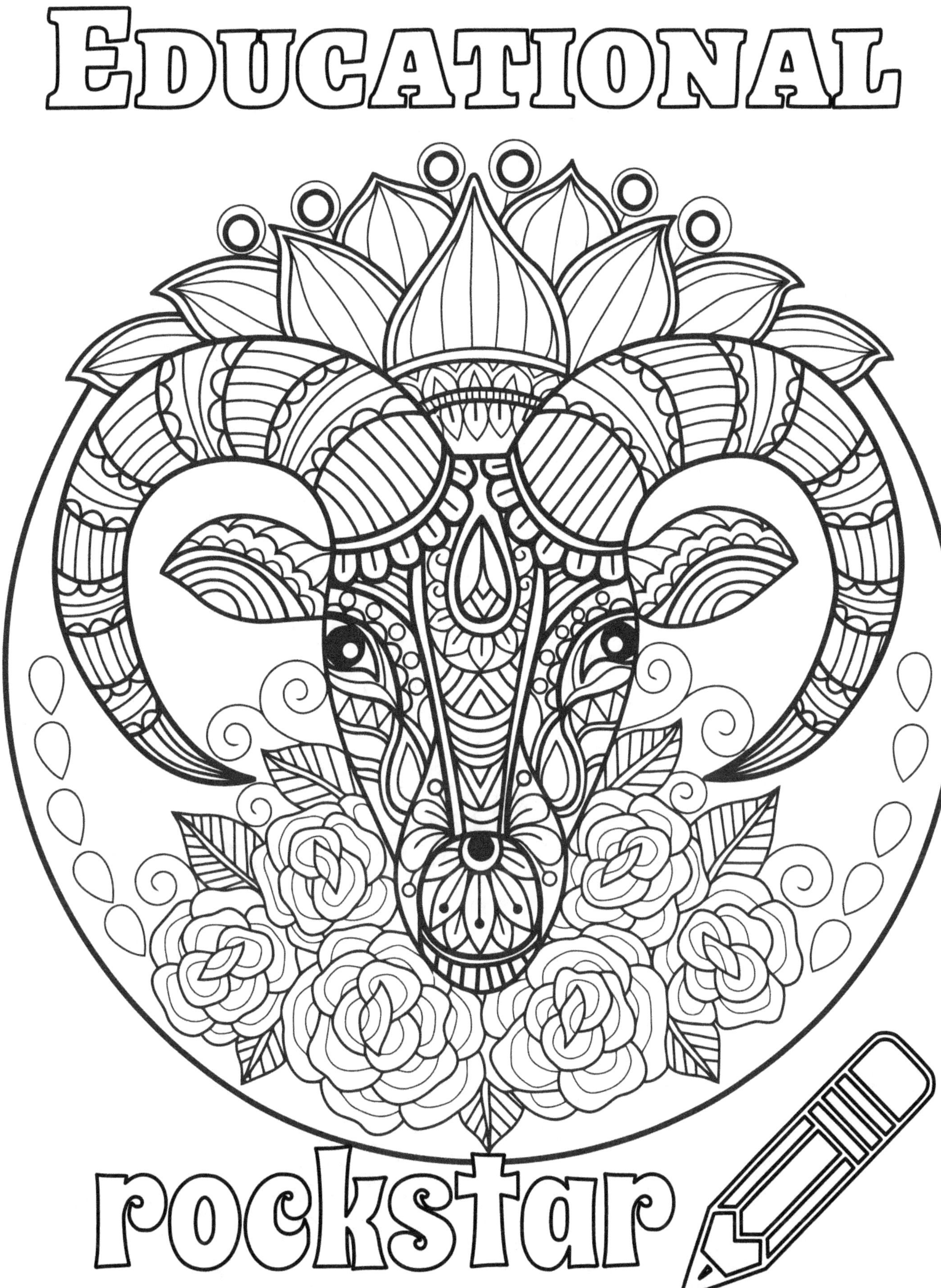
Educational
rockstar

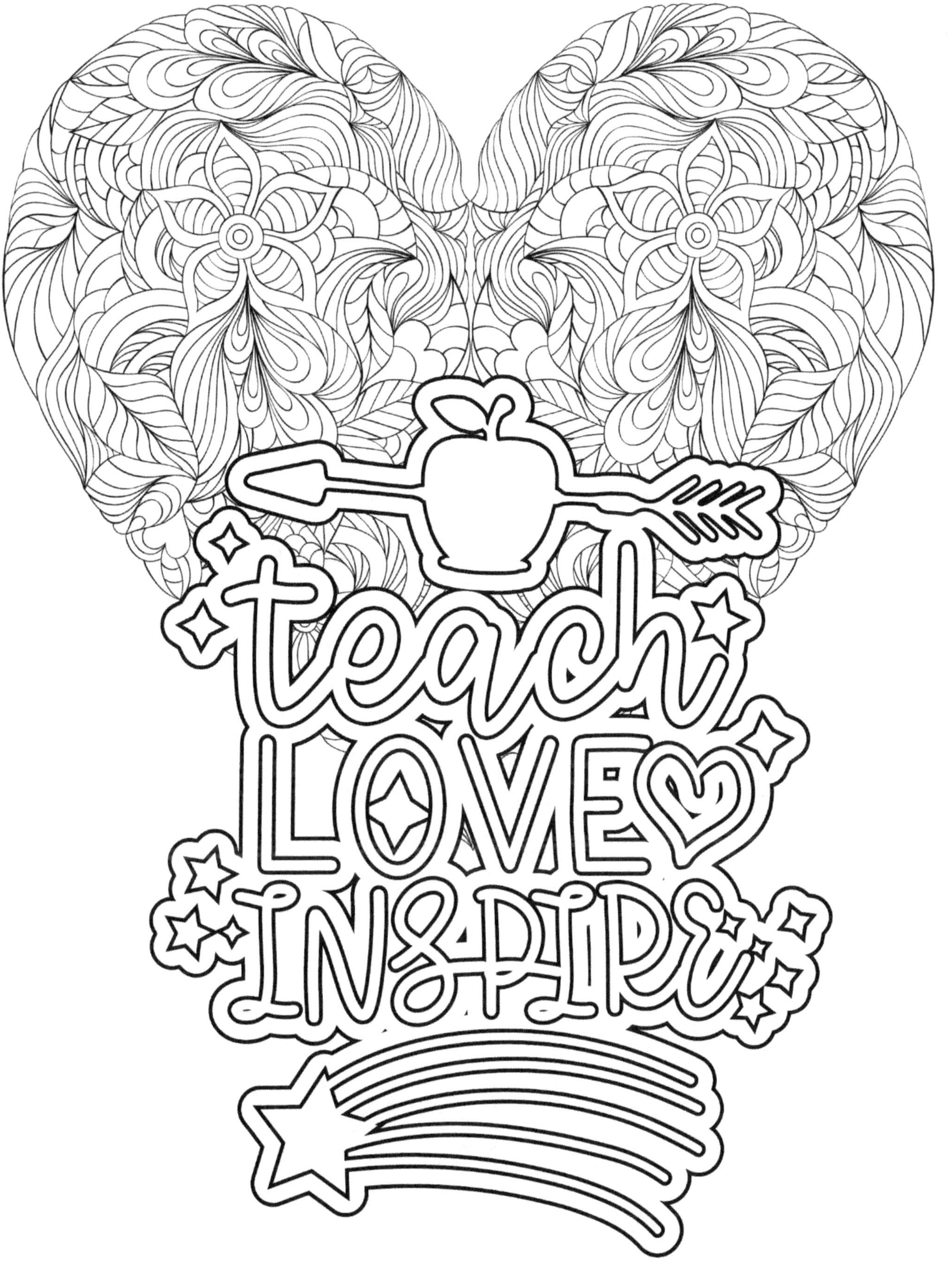
teach
LOVE
INSPIRE

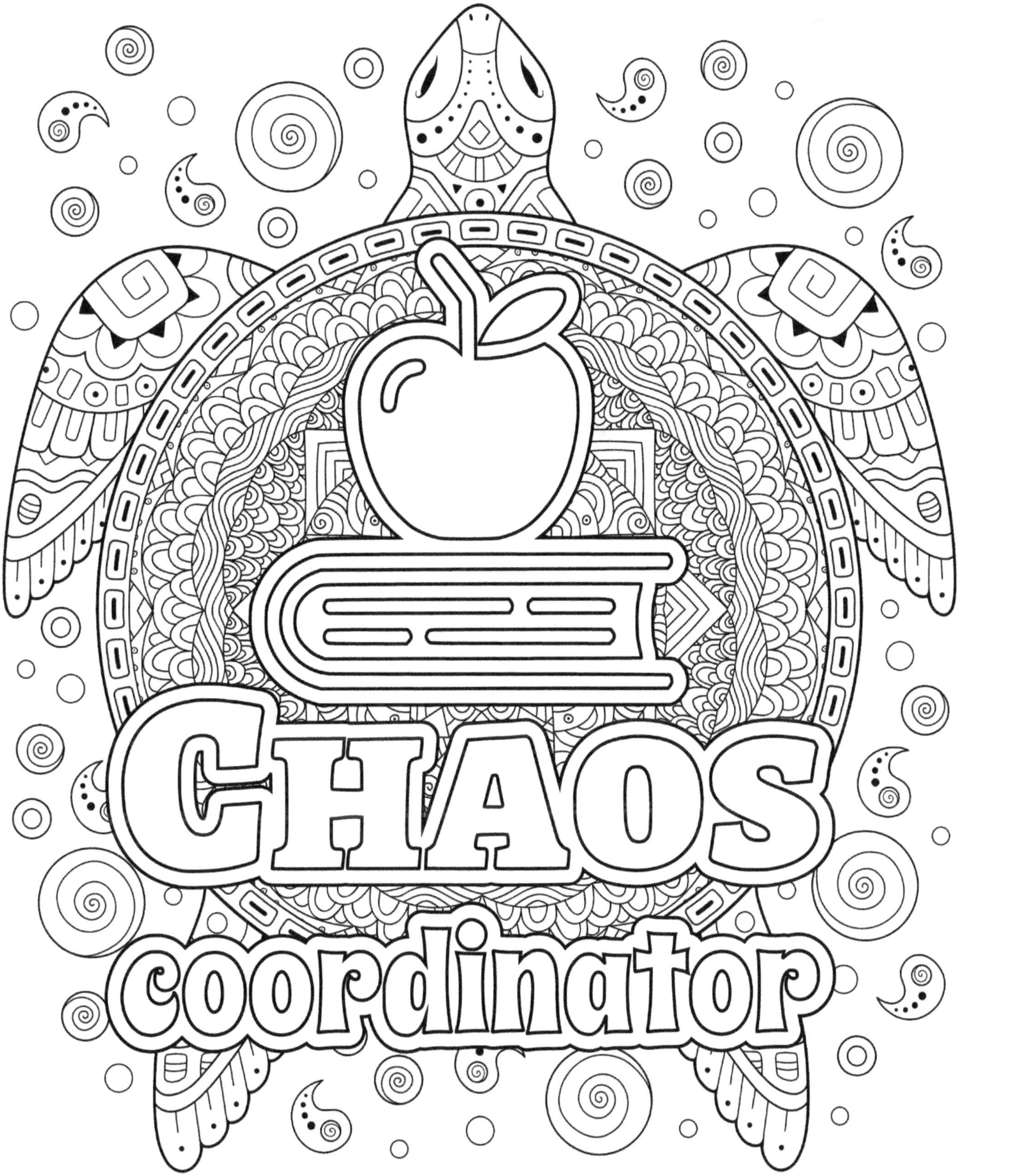
CHAOS
coordinator

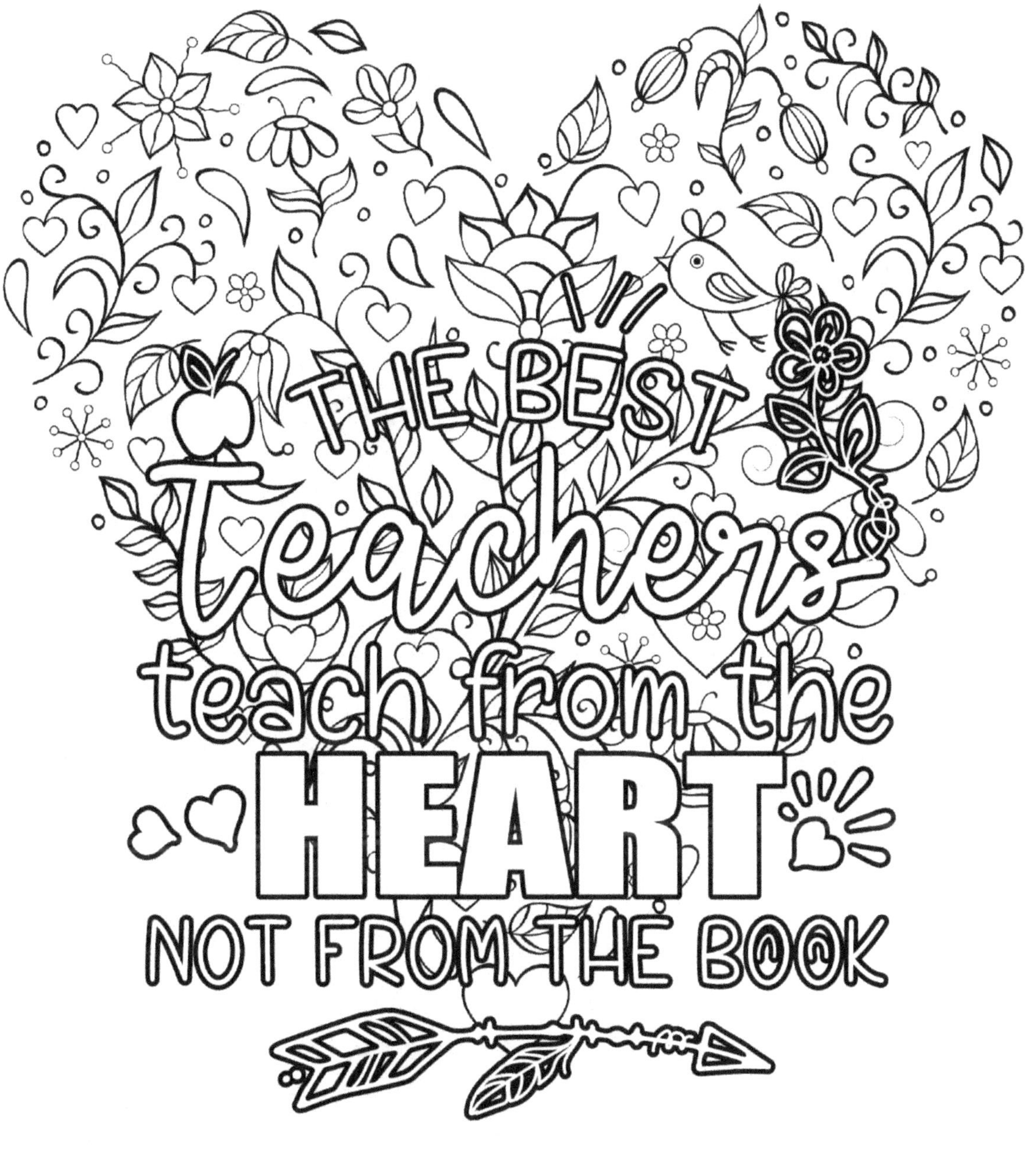
THE BEST
Teachers
teach from the
HEART
NOT FROM THE BOOK

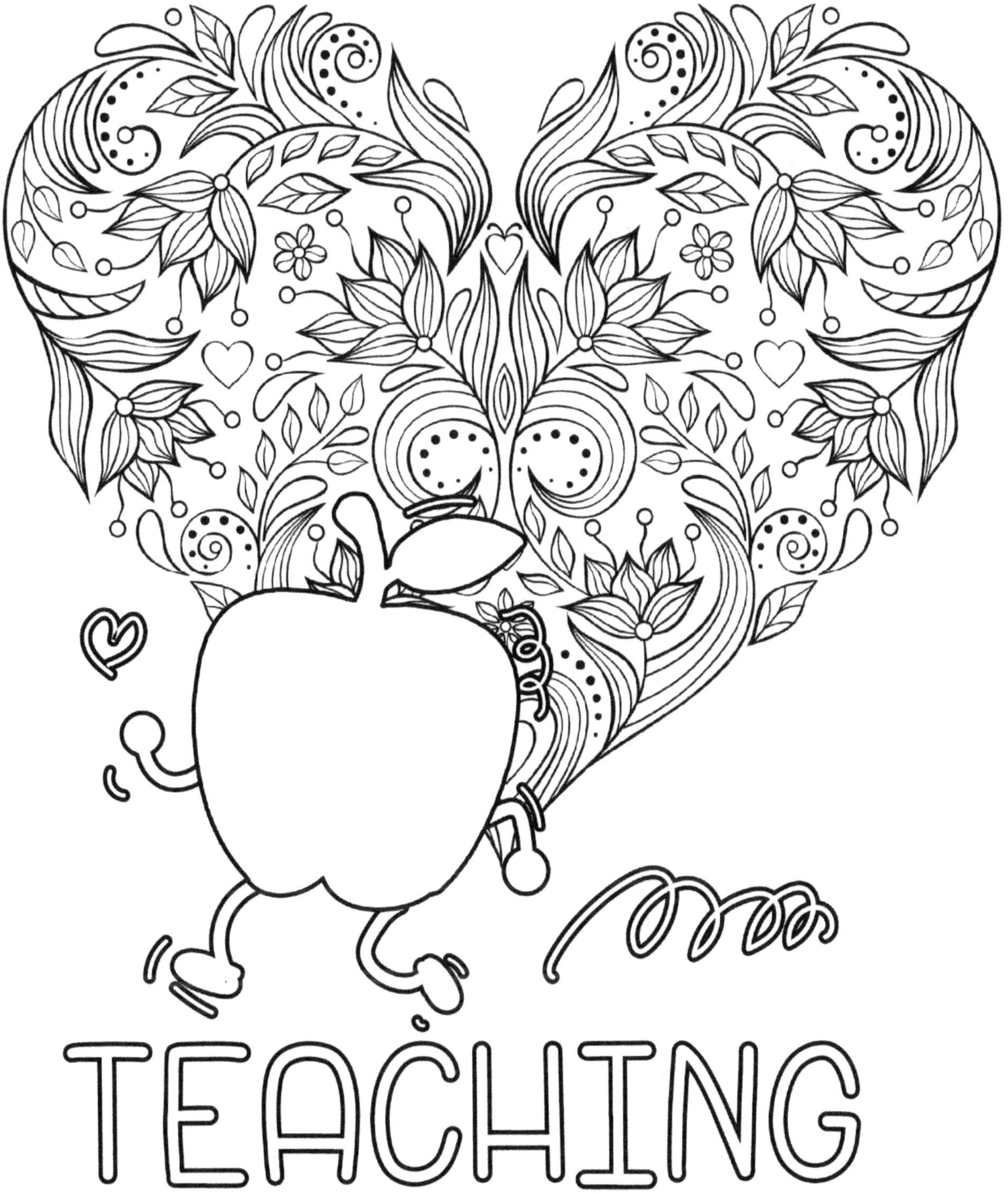

TEACHING IS A WORK OF HEART

www.ingramcontent.com/pod-product-compliance
Lightning Source LLC
Chambersburg PA
CBHW060437220526
45465CB00008B/3177
* 9 7 9 8 5 9 9 5 6 0 0 1 2 *